.99

D1077947

WINSTON CHURCHILL

Statesman or Opportunist?

PETER NEVILLE

Hodder & Stoughton

A MEMBER OF THE HODDER HEADLINE GROUP

Acknowledgements

The publishers would like to thank the following for their permission to reproduce illustrations in this volume:

Chartwell (The National Trust): Courtauld Institute of Art, cover; The Illustrated London News Picture Library, p. 38; Evening Standard, 21st January 1920/Cartoons, University of Kent, p. 39; The Daily Record and Mail, 28th November 1934, p. 66; Hulton-Deutsch, p. 117, p. 131

Every effort has been made to trace and acknowledge ownership of copyright. The publishers will be glad to make suitable arrangements with any copyright holder whom it has not been possible to contact.

British Library Cataloguing in Publication Data
A catalogue for this title is available from the British Library

ISBN 0 340 60664 9

First published 1996
Impression number   10   9   8   7   6   5   4   3   2   1
                     1999   1998   1997   1996

Typeset by Litho Link Ltd, Welshpool, Powys, Wales.
Printed in Great Britain for Hodder & Stoughton Educational, a division of Hodder Headline Plc, 338 Euston Road, London NW1 3BH by Redwood Books, Trowbridge, Wiltshire.

2

CONTENTS

INTRODUCTION

Winston Churchill once remarked at a dinner party, 'I have frequently been forced to eat my words. I have always found them a most nourishing diet!' This, for his critics, might be a consistent pattern throughout his career, with flamboyant and reckless decisions turning into erratic changes – all, it was alleged, the result of a vast ego, and a conviction that he was born under a special star with a special mission to achieve fame.

Churchill was not a party man. It was an underlying theme of his career that he disliked the parliamentary discipline of the House of Commons and sought consensus across party lines. He began his career as a Conservative MP, achieved high office with the Liberals before the First World War only to desert them in turn, and within a couple of years became a Tory Chancellor of the Exchequer. 'Anyone can rat,' Churchill said later, 'it takes courage to re-rat.' This lack of consistency was combined with a lack of antennae where others were concerned. Churchill was so absorbed with his personal ambitions and activities that he tended to forget about others and their needs, a notable characteristic when he was Prime Minister during the Second World War. He could also be rude and abrasive while achieving memorable put-downs and one-liners. 'There but for the grace of God goes God', he said of the rather earnest Sir Stafford Cripps, and when the legendary MP, Nancy Astor, chided him by saying that if she were married to him she would 'poison his coffee', Churchill replied devastatingly, 'Nancy, if I were married to you, I would drink it!' Such cutting ripostes combined with Churchill's boundless ambition made him many enemies. Yet he was constantly surprised by his unpopularity, especially at the time of the Gallipoli fiasco in 1915 (see page 35).

THE SON

Throughout his life, Churchill was haunted by the memory of his father Lord Randolph Churchill who had a glittering career in the 1880s, and became Chancellor of the Exchequer before throwing it all away with a precipitate resignation. There is a poignant quality about young Winston's persistent attempts to attract his father's love and attention, and his failure to do so. He once sadly told his own son, Randolph (after they had had one of their lengthy and often ill-tempered discussions) that he had only one or two conversations of any length with his father in his whole life. Cruel, abrasive letters frequently expressed Lord Randolph's displeasure at his son's behaviour. For his mother, Lady Jennie, there was worship from afar but little intimacy in boyhood. Constant pleadings to visit young Winston at school were rarely acceded to by his parents. The most supportive figure in Churchill's childhood was his nurse Mrs Everest.

What psychological key can Churchill's childhood experience provide for later behaviour? Was it perhaps the cause of his famous 'black dog', the paralysing depression which sometimes used to afflict him? We can only speculate. But the historian Norman Rose writes that: 'Whatever Winston did it was never enough to satisfy his father's exalted standards.' And in old age he could still dream of meeting his father and pointing to his achievements as proof that he was not as Lord Randolph constantly alleged, 'slovenly'. From Lord Randolph, too, Churchill inherited a fear of mortality, that he would die young, and had no time to waste. Contemporaries, whether admirers or critics, could not but notice that Winston Churchill was 'a young man in a hurry'.

THE WARRIOR

Churchill, his colleague and Prime Minister Stanley Baldwin once observed, 'really understands battles'. He joined the army as a young man, fought in the trenches in the First World War, became First Lord of the Admiralty, Air Minister and finally Prime Minister with overall control of Britain's war effort. The martial virtues were the ones he admired most throughout his life, and he gloried in the battlefield.

Here is a passage from Churchill's *My Early Life* where he describes his part in the Battle of Omdurman.

> Suddenly in the midst of the troop up sprung a Dervish. How he got there I do not know. He must have leaped out of some scrub or hole. All the troopers turned upon him thrusting with their lances; but he darted to and fro causing for the moment a frantic commotion. Wounded several times, he staggered towards me raising his spear. I shot him at less than a yard. He fell on the sand, and lay there dead. How easy to kill a man! But I did not worry about it.

A whole chapter in the book is entitled 'The Sensations of a Cavalry Charge'. For many this book epitomised Churchill at his worst. Vainglorious, uncaring about the loss of human life, and delighting in the fame that his exploits brought him. Churchill also claimed to relish the company of military men and implied that they returned the compliment. But this claim is not easily supported. Leading generals like Alanbrooke found Churchill's constant interventions tiresome when he was Prime Minister, and naval officers found him irksome when he ran the Admiralty between 1911 and 1915. Far from being an admirer of Churchill, Sir David Beatty, the most famous battle-cruiser commander in the First World War, loathed him. In 1917 Beatty wrote of the former Chief of the Royal Navy:

> It is of course useless to expect a man such as he to do anything but intrigue and he has evidently made use of, or is attempting to make use of a certain feeling that has been put about that the Navy ought to be doing more.

Shortly afterwards Beatty accused Churchill of being 'devoid of real patriotism'. It is difficult to sustain Beatty's charge but it is interesting that an admiral of the fleet felt obliged to make it.

Churchill also had military obsessions which could be costly. One of these in the Second World War was his belief that Italy was 'the soft underbelly of the Axis'. He endowed the Italian campaign of 1943–5, in the words of one historian, with an 'almost mystical quality', and resisted American demands that France, not the Mediterranean, should be the main theatre of the war (see p. 118). Throughout his life he craved action and excitement and confessed to feeling bored in 1945 when the war was over.

THE STATESMAN

Rashness and impetuosity are not good servants for a statesman of international renown. Yet Churchill was frequently accused of reacting emotionally and pulling political rabbits out of a hat like a magician. His colleague Neville Chamberlain thought Churchill a 'brilliant creature' and 'a man of tremendous drive and imagination', but that talking to him was like talking to 'a brass band'. When in government he constantly interfered in the running of other departments, even more so when he was in overall control between 1940 and 1945. He was more emollient as a peacetime Prime Minister between 1951 and 1955 offering 'a quiet, steady administration', but his penchant for cross-party appointments using Liberals, or even men with no clear affiliations, was as clear as ever.

In the sphere of foreign affairs, Churchill was closely linked with the events surrounding the post-war settlement in Europe in 1944–5. He admired Stalin – 'I like that man' – but did he allow himself to be hoodwinked in the infamous 'naughty document' of 1944 and the subsequent agreement at Yalta in February 1945? By 1948 the whole of Eastern Europe had, to use Churchill's own phrase, fallen behind 'an iron curtain'. Controversy continues about Churchill's role in the origins of the Cold War.

Churchill set his face against decolonisation saying that he had not become Prime Minister of Britain to preside over the 'liquidation of the British Empire', and in the 1930s cast himself into a political limbo because of his total refusal to contemplate the concession of independence to India. This was why President Roosevelt and other American leaders regarded him as an arch-imperialist and a Victorian relic (a fact that Churchill wryly acknowledged himself). And yet Churchill is accused by John Charmley in *The End of Glory* of deliberately forcing Britain into a war for which it was not ready, so handing over Eastern Europe to Soviet domination and precipitating the collapse of the Empire he so cherished.

1

YOUNG WINSTON

Winston Leonard Spencer Churchill was born in 1874 at Blenheim Palace. On his paternal side, he was descended both from the first Earl Spencer and John Churchill, first Duke of Marlborough, the Commander-in-Chief of the allied armies that had inflicted a series of severe defeats on the French in the war of the Spanish Succession. Blenheim itself was named after the first and most famous of the great Duke's victories in 1704.

A son, therefore, of the British aristocracy, Winston Churchill had an unusual trait for his class and time. His mother Jennie Jerome was an American, the daughter of a rich and successful stockbroker, financier and newspaper owner, and the mature Churchill always remained proud of the transatlantic connection. Yet the relationship with his mother was in many ways a remote one. Churchill was to write later that 'she shone for me like the Evening Star. I loved her dearly but at "a distance".' Beautiful and vivacious though she was, Jennie Jerome seemed to take scant interest in her sons' lives (a second son Jack was born after Winston). For Winston in particular, the family nanny Everest, or 'Woomany' as he called her, was a much more potent influence than his mother as Churchill himself was the first to admit. 'It was to her,' he said, 'that I poured out my many troubles.' He remained devoted to her until her death in 1892, was present at her deathbed and told his mother rather pathetically, 'I shall never know such a friend again.' Historians have speculated about the effects of such maternal deprivation on Winston Churchill's life. It was obviously significant, but it needs to be remembered that remote parents and loving (or not so loving) nannies were a common feature of upper-class Victorian life in England.

Winston's relationship with his father, Lord Randolph Churchill, was even more difficult. For much of Winston's childhood and adolescence,

Lord Randolph proved to be a censorious, authoritarian and permanently absent parent. Only right at the end of his life did Winston's father show any real interest in his son, when he asked him to forgive a tendency to 'speak roughly in sudden annoyance'. It says much for Winston's admiration for his father (this being one of only three or four occasions in his life when he had a long and intimate conversation with Lord Randolph) that he forgave the many slights and gibes he suffered at his hands so readily. He did not know until many years later that Lord Randolph was suffering from the agonizing terminal symptoms of syphilis which sharpened a tendency to have violent mood swings. Later in his life, Winston too was to suffer from a tendency towards depression which he famously called his 'black dog'.

It was from his father that Winston was to get his obsession with politics. And it was the shattering crash of Lord Randolph's political career in 1886 which provided the spur for Winston to enter the political arena. Lord Randolph was MP for Woodstock and rapidly rose up what Disraeli called the 'greasy pole' of politics to the Cabinet. In the Conservative government of 1886 Churchill was given the post of Chancellor of the Exchequer, and the historian Paul Addison has noted that he would almost certainly have succeeded the then Prime Minister, Lord Salisbury, had he not been 'too frantic and unstable to wait'. Instead, Churchill chose to take on the Secretary of State for War and the First Lord of the Admiralty over the issue of cuts in the arms estimates, and when they would not agree, he wrote to Salisbury asking to be 'allowed to give up my office and retire from the Government'.

Lord Randolph has not received sympathetic treatment from historians. He espoused causes like protectionism only to drop them shortly afterwards, and his cynical playing of the 'Orange Card' over Irish Home Rule (coining the phrase 'Ulster will fight, Ulster will be right' to encourage Protestant opposition to Home Rule) earned him the undying hatred of Parnell and the Irish Nationalists who had originally believed him to be an ally. His son was to have an equally chequered record over Irish affairs. Like Winston, Lord Randolph has frequently been charged with opportunism. No one was ever quite sure what his catch phrase of 'Tory Democracy' meant and Paul Addison's assessment, though harsh, is hard to refute. 'He was', Addison concludes, 'a supremely tactical politician in whose career it was difficult to see anything beyond the calculation of short-term personal advantage.'

However, for his son Winston, Lord Randolph's fall was the central, traumatic event of his entire life. Frequently accused by political opponents of lack of consistency, Winston never wavered in his admiration for his father (which was never reciprocated), nor in his fierce determination to carry through what he saw as his father's political legacy.

SCHOOL DAYS

Winston was rather unhappy at preparatory school, constantly pleading for parental visits which rarely occurred. He was accused (among other things) of being unable 'to quite understand the meaning of hard work'. But he did well enough to secure entrance to Harrow School in 1887. His first reaction was favourable. 'I like everything immensely' he wrote in his first letter from Harrow to his parents. However, his lateness, and talent for losing books and papers were such an irritant to an unfortunate Harrow master that he complained to Lady Randolph that 'he is so regular in his irregularity that I really don't know what to do: and sometimes think he cannot help it'.

But there was another side to the slovenly schoolboy. Quite early in his Harrow career, Winston won a prize for reciting 1000 lines of 'The Lays of Ancient Rome' word-perfect, and he was a regular winner of form history prizes as well as becoming public schools' fencing champion. None of this unduly impressed Lord Randolph though, and he decided that Winston was not intelligent enough to go to university and must join the army. Years later, Churchill was to ruefully remark that at the time he believed that his father had recognised him as 'a military genius'. The truth was more mundane and unflattering, and Winston was forced to join the 'Army Class' at Harrow. This was for boys intended for a service career and bored young Churchill because of its narrow curriculum.

Churchill's last months at Harrow were fraught with anxiety. Twice in 1892 he failed the entrance exams for the Royal Military Academy at Sandhurst and Lord Randolph threatened him with that ultimately distasteful fate, a career in business. After a further period in a crammer for the sons of the rich, he passed the Sandhurst exams in August 1893. His marks were not quite good enough for infantry training, so Winston was to begin his service career in the cavalry.

THE MILITARY EXPERIENCE

—

Any pleasure that Winston derived from passing into Sandhurst was dulled by a savage letter from his father who was now severely affected by the symptoms of his disease which began to affect his sanity. 'Never', wrote Lord Randolph with exaggerated venom, 'have I received a really good report of your conduct in work from any master or tutor you had from time to time to do with.' Continuing in a tone which almost suggested that his son had failed to get into Sandhurst, Lord Randolph warned, 'Do not think I am going to take the trouble of writing you long letters after every folly and failure you commit.' Not surprisingly Winston Churchill, in the words of his biographer Martin Gilbert, was 'crushed by the rebuke'.

Winston found the regime at Sandhurst tougher than anything he had experienced at school. But he had a natural affinity with rifles and artillery pieces, military history and tactics. Mrs Everest fretted about an over-active social life with 'late hours and late dinners', but it did not detract from his studies.

Winston and his brother Jack had a narrow escape from death in 1894 on holiday in Switzerland when they almost drowned after a boating trip. This, and a number of other experiences, gave him an acute awareness of mortality which was sharpened when Lord Randolph died in January 1895. He was only forty-six years old, and his premature death (and that of his uncle also in his forties) convinced Winston that he would die young. 'Is it forty and finished?' Churchill was to ask. Only in 1967, Martin Gilbert points out, did Churchill's own son publish evidence that showed conclusively that his grandfather had died from syphilis and not an hereditary disease. This was two years after Winston Churchill's own death.

timeline	1874	Churchill born
	1887	Enters Harrow School
	1893	Enters Royal Military Academy, Sandhurst
	1895	Death of Lord Randolph Churchill

2

ASPIRING POLITICIAN

Four weeks after his father's death, Winston Churchill was commissioned into the army as a second lieutenant in the Fourth Hussars, in charge of a squad of about 30 men. At the outset of his career as a serving officer, Winston was strangely unsettled. Increasingly his thoughts turned towards politics and as they did so, he became more and more conscious of the defects in his own rather narrow military education. And yet, even at this stage he was capable of perceptive political judgement. In 1895 the Liberals were defeated at the polls and replaced by a Conservative and Unionist government (those former Liberals who had joined the Tories over the issue of Irish Home Rule were called Unionists). Churchill was cautious about their prospects. They were, he declared, 'too brilliant altogether. They are just the sort of government to split on the question of Protection.' Ten years later, the Tory government was indeed to be split on the issue of tariff protection and go down to a catastrophic defeat. Churchill was to play a part in its demise.

In the interim Churchill visited his mother's homeland, the United States, which impressed him. He also reported on the Spanish-American war in Cuba for the *Daily Graphic*, so beginning a lifelong involvement with journalism.

INDIA

Dull reality intervened. Churchill's regiment was due to be sent to India, a development which the young adventurer did not find the least bit attractive. Once there he tried, through Lady Randolph's influence, to secure a posting with Lord Kitchener's army in Egypt which was about to deal with a native revolt in the Sudan. But this effort failed. Winston then told his mother about a long-term intention to leave the army and become an MP. This enraged Lady Randolph who tartly informed him that he seemed to 'have no real purpose in life'.

With his mother's criticism ringing in his ears, Winston remained in India although he took advantage of a leave in London to seek medical advice about a lisp which made him pronounce 's' as 'sh'. No organic defect was found and the lisp never fully disappeared, but it did not impede the rise of the future politician and House of Commons orator.

During this leave in 1897, Churchill also made a request to Conservative Party Central Office to arrange a speaking tour for him. At 22, Lord Randolph's son made his first political speech to an audience near Bath praising his father's concept of 'Tory Democracy', and deriding those 'croakers' who thought that the British Empire was in decline. A capacity for using the vivid phrase was already evident. British workmen, Winston informed his audience, could expect more 'from the rising tide of Tory Democracy than from the dried-up drainpipe of Radicalism'. He was gratified by a favourable report on his speech in the *Morning Post.*

THE NORTH-WEST FRONTIER

Back in India, boredom set in once more as Churchill diverted himself by growing roses and writing a novel. The chance of action against the fierce tribesmen on India's north-west frontier then arose, but Churchill's attempt to substitute for an officer killed in action failed. So, on the advice of the commanding British officer on the frontier, he got himself accredited as a correspondent of the *Daily Telegraph*. Observers of young Churchill's career might have been forgiven for asking whether the young man was a soldier or a journalist, and been surprised at the indulgence with which the Army allowed such a young officer to set off on such escapades.

Churchill's experiences with the Malakand Field Force, and his comments on them, afford interesting insights into his personality and attitudes. There was a desire for glory with Winston telling his brother Jack that there was 'no ambition I cherish so keenly as to gain a reputation of personal courage'. This was combined with an apparent egomania which many people found extremely distasteful. 'I am so conceited,' he confided to his mother, 'that I do not believe that the gods would create so potent a being as myself for so prosaic an ending.' The reference to 'the gods' is significant. He had already given up all Christian belief in favour of belief in a personal fate, but one which was special, a feeling which sustained him all his life.

There is no doubt that Churchill was a brave soldier. He was involved in some desperate actions against the native tribesmen where no mercy was shown and none expected (both sides routinely killed their opponents' wounded). He was mentioned in despatches and awarded medals for his conduct, and clearly gloried in the publicity which this brought to him. Yet there was always another softer, more reflective side to Churchill's character. In thinking about the frontier war, he wished that he could 'come to the conclusion that all this barbarity – all these losses – all this expenditure – had resulted in a permanent settlement being obtained'. Unusually, for an army officer, Churchill did not want expenditure on the Army to be increased. Instead (and appropriately perhaps for a future First Lord of the Admiralty), he wanted Britain to rely for its defence on a so-called 'two-power standard' navy – one which would be twice as big as that of any rival.

The journalist in Churchill also saw a publishing opportunity in recounting his military experiences on the north-west frontier. He kept careful notes and corresponded with fellow officers to get details of their experiences. The result was a book entitled *The Story of the Malakand Field Force* which Winston Churchill managed to place with a publisher within a week – though only with the help of his mother. She persuaded the Conservative politician Arthur Balfour to contact his own literary agent to get a publisher for the book.

THE SUDAN CAMPAIGN

Ever seeking action, Winston Churchill now again attempted to get himself attached to Lord Kitchener's army in the Sudan which was involved in putting down a long-standing revolt by Dervish tribesmen. In the meantime he continued to press his political ambitions by making a speech at Bradford which he had some hopes of representing as a Conservative MP. The speech – which Churchill described as 'the greatest pleasure of my life' – was well received and was followed shortly afterwards by a meeting with the then Prime Minister, Lord Salisbury. The man who had been instrumental in bringing an end to his father's political career told Winston Churchill how much he reminded him of his father and promised his help if it was needed in the future. Churchill was quick to take up this offer by getting Salisbury's backing for his effort to join Kitchener's army. Lady Randolph also wrote to Kitchener but it needed the additional intervention of the Adjutant-General before Churchill secured his posting, without attachment to a newspaper.

Thus it was that Churchill witnessed and took part in the British Army's last great cavalry action against the Dervishes at Omdurman. Predictably, superior British technology secured a victory despite the reckless courage of the tribesmen, but Churchill was shocked by the treatment of the wounded Dervishes after the battle. The victory, he wrote, was disgraced by 'the inhuman slaughter of the wounded' for which, he believed, 'Kitchener was responsible'. He followed this up with a book about the campaign in the Sudan called *The River War* which again castigated Kitchener. Churchill was especially critical of the destruction of the tomb of the Mahdi after which his corpse was dug up (the Mahdi, self-styled descendant of the Prophet Muhammad, had instigated the Sudanese uprising in the 1880s). This, said Churchill, in a phrase which infuriated Kitchener, 'was a wicked act of which the true Christian, no less than the philosopher, must express his abhorrence'.

The *Morning Post* paid Churchill £200 for his letters on the Sudan campaign and he went back to India for a final period before leaving the Army. He returned to England in March 1899 never to see India again, although various preconceptions about the sub-continent and the inevitability of British rule remained with him for most of his life.

He then stood as Tory candidate for Oldham in a by-election and tried to promote his father's policies on Irish Home Rule and the preservation of the British Empire.

In foreign and imperial affairs, Churchill was also his father's son. The Empire must be preserved and with it 'command of the seas'. Unfortunately the electors of Oldham could not be persuaded to elect Churchill Junior on this occasion. His defeat was narrow. He was congratulated on his efforts by Arthur Balfour (soon to be Prime Minister himself) who looked forward to the day when Winston would join him on the parliamentary benches where 'your father and I fought many a good battle'. Lord Salisbury wrote privately to Lady Randolph saying that 'Winston made a splendid fight'. A young man in a hurry needed powerful patrons in the Conservative Party.

SOUTH AFRICA

In the meantime a new colonial crisis had arisen in South Africa where the Dutch-speaking Afrikaners (or Boers) in the Transvaal objected to the increasing flow of so-called *Uitlanders* (foreigners) into their republic, and the British demand that they be extended voting rights. War between the Afrikaners and the British appeared imminent in the autumn of 1899, and Winston Churchill was attracted as ever by the sound of gunfire. He got himself accredited as the *Daily Mail* correspondent with the princely salary of £1000 for a four-month posting (£40,000 in 1990s' value), and was in South Africa when the first shots of the Second Boer War were fired in October 1899.

Churchill's time in South Africa was dominated by one dramatic episode. This was when an armoured train on which he was travelling was ambushed by the Boers and he was captured after an heroic defence in which he played a leading role. The Boers took Churchill to a prison in Pretoria, and rejected his pleas that he was a journalist and not a soldier. One of the Boer commanders pointed out, not unreasonably, that the Englishman had organised the defence of the armoured train and was 'one of the most dangerous prisoners in our hands'. But Churchill was not prepared to sit out the war in a Boer prison. He soon escaped, hid down a mineshaft and eventually crossed by train into Portuguese East Africa despite the efforts of the Boers to recapture him. This adventure made Winston Churchill a national hero and a popular music hall song of the day dubbed him 'the latest and the greatest correspondent of the day'.

THE NEW MP FOR OLDHAM

In July 1900, Churchill returned to England and within days he had been rapturously adopted as the Conservative candidate for Oldham in the imminent general election. Yet, surprisingly perhaps, given the jingoistic atmosphere of the general election of 1900 (held in the middle of the

Boer War), Churchill's election victory was as narrow as his by-election defeat had been in 1899 (the margin was only 221 votes). But his victory was hailed on all sides of the political spectrum. The Secretary of State for War wrote to congratulate him saying that no one 'who ever got into Parliament has done more than you have done in the last two years to entitle him to represent a constituency'.

Winston Churchill had, therefore, achieved his initial ambition to sit on those same parliamentary benches which his father had dominated for so brief a span less than two decades before. Brave, talented, generous; he was all these things but in his rush to the top Churchill also showed a capacity for ruthless ambition and limitless self-advertisement. Robert Rhodes James' verdict on the young aspirant politician may be somewhat harsh but it is not unjust. Churchill, writes James, was never afraid to risk his own life, 'but the accusations far from unmerited – that he was an adventurer and a medal-hunter – dimmed the very real and substantial military, literary and political achievements that stood to his credit'. A kinder contemporary comment by A.G. Gardiner, the editor of the Liberal *Daily News* in 1908, noted that Winston Churchill never tried to conceal this ambition:

> To the insatiable curiosity and enthusiasm of the child he joints the frankness of the child. He has no reserves and no shame. You are welcome to anything he has, and may pry into any corner you like. He has that scorn of concealment that belongs to a caste which never doubts itself.

It was this very certainty, the sureness that he had been selected for a special fate, that could antagonise political allies and opponents alike.

timeline	1895	Passes out of Sandhurst
	1898	Battle of Omdurman
	1899	Churchill defeated in Oldham by-election
	1900	Churchill captured by Boers but escapes. Elected Conservative MP for Oldham

3

THE RADICAL REFORMER

Winston Churchill made his maiden speech in the House of Commons on 28 February 1900. It pleased his political leaders with its support for the war effort against the Boers. 'We have no cause', the young MP told his listeners, 'to be ashamed of anything that has passed during the war.' There was the now customary reference too to the 'splendid memory' of Lord Randolph. Press reaction was effusive. The *Daily Express* found young Churchill's speech 'spell-binding' while the *Daily Telegraph* praised his 'sparkling sentences'. Only the *Daily Chronicle* referred rather meanly to the 'unfortunate lisp in his voice'.

CHURCHILL'S DEFECTION

With the powerful patronage of men like Balfour and Joseph Chamberlain, Churchill should have had a golden future in the Tory Party. Yet, within four years he had crossed the floor of the House of Commons to join the Liberals and would soon become a Liberal Cabinet minister, hated and reviled by his Tory opponents.

It is tempting to see this development, as many Conservatives did at the time, as a result of naked ambition. Churchill certainly found the humble role of a backbench MP irksome. It was impossible, he wrote, for the ordinary MP to 'influence in the slightest degree the policy of a powerful government'. Rhodes James, among other commentators, recognises the role that ambition played in Churchill's decision to leave the Tory Party in 1904. 'He wanted to get on,' writes James. 'He thought himself held back in the Conservative ranks. He was, like his father, in a hurry.' But Churchill did disagree with the Conservative leaders on a number of issues, notably free trade and protection. Even before Joseph Chamberlain began his great campaign in favour of protection in 1902, Martin Gilbert points out, Churchill made a speech attacking it and defending the merits of Britain's traditional free trade policy. And like his father, Churchill attacked plans for increased military expenditure as excessive, accusing Balfour of allowing government expenditure to 'get beyond the point of prudence and reason'.

Well before his decision to abandon the Tories, the young man was cultivating ties with the so-called 'Liberal Imperialists' like Lord Roseberry (that is, those Liberals who had, unlike the non-conformist wing of the party, supported the Tory position over South Africa). This development was significant, for a consistent theme in Churchill's career was to be his restless dissatisfaction with party labels and party discipline. Even if we put aside his declaration in 1903, 'I hate the Tory Party' as a reflection of youthful revolt, it has to be recognised nonetheless that Churchill was never a good party man. In his talks with Roseberry, who became a personal friend, Churchill referred ehthusiastically to

> the Government of the Middle – the party which shall be free at once from the sordid selfishness and callousness of Toryism at one end, and the blind appetite of the Radical masses at the other.

Much later in his career he would be found pining for the simplicity of coalition non-party government and frustrated by the dogmatic certainties of party warfare. But he also maintained a persistent fear of the growing Labour movement – hence the coded reference to the 'blind appetite of the Radical masses'. Sound coalition government should be an alliance of reasonable Tories and Liberals. The political demise of the Liberals after the First World War obviously presented Churchill with a problem.

The difficulty with Churchill's rhetoric in his early years, as throughout his career, is which came first, conviction or ambition? Were the flowing words and the dramatic turns of phrase, in Paul Addison's words, 'a magnificent façade of sham statesmanship' or a vehicle for assisting him to bring about change in British society? Historians have reached no firm decision on this issue. In the end, we are left with Addison's question about Winston Churchill still echoing: 'Was he, in the final analysis, a kind of glittering parasite on the surface of society?'

Whatever his motives, it is clear that Churchill became increasingly disenchanted with Toryism from 1902 onwards. When Joseph Chamberlain began his great campaign to convert his party to protection, his old ally's son denounced it as a 'fantastic policy' and formed the 'Free Food League' with like-minded Tory MPs. So fierce were his attacks on protectionism, with references to tariffs as 'quack remedies', that when Arthur Balfour reshuffled his Conservative government in September 1903, Churchill was excluded from any hope of office, according to Martin Gilbert, because his 'Free Trade views were too extreme'. This may have marked the real parting of the ways between Winston Churchill and his father's party. He had already endangered his position as MP for protectionist Oldham where the cotton mill owners favoured tariffs against foreign competition, and was known to be receiving offers from Liberal constituencies to stand in the forthcoming general election (one came from his Liberal uncle, Lord Tweedsmuir). On 31 December 1903, Churchill further outraged mainstream Tories by lunching with the most hated representative of the radical Liberals, David Lloyd George. During the Boer War when Churchill was patriotism personified, Lloyd George had narrowly escaped being torn to pieces by a pro-war mob for supporting the Boers in their struggle (he had to be smuggled out of Birmingham Town Hall disguised as a policeman!).

Three months later, Churchill had become so unpopular in the Tory Party that when he rose to launch another attack on protection in the House of Commons, the entire parliamentary party (save a few Free Traders) walked out of the chamber in symbolic protest. Further humiliation followed in April 1904 when Churchill, who relied on a formidable memory to learn his speeches by heart, forgot his lines and was forced to sit down. Older MPs were uncomfortably reminded of Lord Randolph's last pathetic, illness-stricken efforts to speak in the House, but his son learnt a lesson from this disaster. In future, although carefully rehearsed, he never went into the Commons without copious notes to refer to. It is an historical irony that a politician who is remembered as one of Britain's great orators, never developed the capacity to think on his feet. All Churchill's oratory was a product of laborious preparation and rehearsal.

One factor alone obstructed Churchill's long expected defection to the Liberals in 1904. This was the issue of Irish Home Rule. It was, after all, Lord Randolph who had coined the divisive slogan 'Ulster will fight, and Ulster will be right!' in the 1880s. But slowly Winston Churchill abandoned his father's position as part of the process of conversion to Liberalism. To begin with he was in favour of what he called 'Administrative Home Rule' whereby Ireland was to be run by provincial councils which would be empowered to set rates, run the railways and administer education in local areas. Later, Churchill would move all the way to acceptance of the principle of a separate Irish parliament in Dublin. On 31 May 1904 he felt able to cross the floor to the Liberal benches in a dramatic gesture and sit down next to his new ally Lloyd George, in the same seat Lord Randolph had occupied during his years of opposition to Gladstone.

THE LIBERAL REFORMER

Winston Churchill had an impressive record as a social reformer. At the Colonial Office (where he was Under Secretary) he showed compassion for the defeated Boers and deserved a good deal of credit for winning their co-operation in the aftermath of the South African War. This compassionate streak was also evident in Churchill's period both as President of the Board of Trade and Home Secretary.

His constructive record was particularly remarkable at the Board of Trade. He presided over the establishment of labour exchanges (1909), measures to curb abuses in the 'sweated' trades like textiles, the Miners' Accidents Act (1910) and the Coal Mines Act (1911). Rhodes James notes that all these measures, though partly the work of specialist advisers and civil servants, owed much to Churchill's 'direct intervention and energy'.

The Struggle Over the People's Budget

The reforming Liberal programme (involving increased expenditure on old age pensions, for example) and the increased naval expenditure in response to a perceived German naval threat meant that a budget deficit of £16.5 million was projected for the financial year 1909–10. But Lloyd George, as Chancellor of the Exchequer, proposed to deal with this eventuality by introducing land taxes and a more steeply graduated income tax. A so-called 'supertax' of an extra 6d in the pound would be imposed on incomes over £5000 per annum. Lloyd George also proposed to increase death duties by a third, and to raise the taxes on liquor licences and spirits. There were also to be new taxes on petrol and motor cars.

As a member of the landed artistocracy, Winston Churchill might have been expected to object to such radical reform (his cousin 'Sunny' was, after all, Duke of Marlborough, and he had been born in the ancestral Churchill home at Blenheim). Indeed, according to Clive Ponting's recent biography Churchill had in fact 'opposed the idea of a radical budget from the start'. However, this squares oddly with Paul Addison's statement that there is 'no documentary evidence that he opposed the radical thrust of the budget'. Neither does it accord with the views of other historians, or find any echo in what Churchill was saying at the time when the so-called 'People's Budget' was fiercely attacked by the Conservative Party and the House of Lords. The Tories were dismissed by Churchill as 'old doddering peers, cute financial magnates, clever wire pullers and big brewers with bulbous noses', and the Lords were contemptuously labelled 'heaven born and God-granted legislators' sitting in their 'prejudiced chamber, hereditary, non-elected, irresponsible and irremediable'. When every allowance is made for accusations of careerism and opportunism against Churchill this hardly seems the language of a man who was resolutely opposed to 'a radical budget from the outset'.

Addison suggests that Churchill's radicalism was tempered only by a desire to protect the social order which he believed would be strengthened by a concession to 'social justice' and his adherence to the fashionable concept of 'national efficiency' which he believed was not assisted by the state of the 'dwindling and cramped villages of our denuded countryside'. Churchill had also gone to some trouble to learn the economic case for the 'People's Budget'. When Tories claimed that the budget was anti-capitalist, he pointed out that it would discriminate between the profits of enterprise and investment and the unearned income coming from inheritance and passive ownership of land. In a speech in September 1909 Churchill posed the question, 'We do not only ask today, "How much have you got?" We also ask "How did you get it? Did you earn it by yourself, or has it just been left to you by others?"' None of these questions endeared him to his own class.

As it was, the quarrel with the House of Lords widened to the greater constitutional issue of whether the Lords, with its in-built Tory majority, had the right to defeat money bills and hamstring the economic management of the country. Without a budget, the country's government could not continue. Two general elections in 1910 which gave the Liberals wafer-thin majorities did little to resolve the issue, by forcing them to rely on the support of Labour and the Irish Nationalists.

The Irish Question Again

The Liberal government was now forced to agree to address once more the question of Irish Home Rule which had laid dormant since Gladstone's Second Home Rule Bill had been defeated in the House of Lords in 1893. As long as the House of Lords had a veto on legislation Home Rule could never come about, but without the promise of Home Rule the Irish would not give the Liberals the votes needed to pass the Parliament Act which would stop the Lords from using their veto against a money bill.

The Parliament Act was duly passed in 1911 which prevented the House of Lords from ever interfering with money bills again, and secured the passage of the 'People's Budget'. But the price of Irish Home Rule had to be paid if the Liberals were to remain in power (the second 1910 election gave them only 272 seats, exactly the same as the Tories). In January 1911 Asquith set up a Cabinet committee on Home Rule of which Churchill was a member. Various options presented themselves.

The first was the old Gladstonian solution which had failed in 1893, which would have given the Irish a separate parliament but with continued representation in the Westminster Parliament. This was open to the objection that it would give Irish MPs a right to vote on British affairs while Welsh, Scots and English MPs would have no say in Irish ones. A second option was 'Home Rule All Round', the solution put forward by Lord Randolph's old ally Joe Chamberlain in 1886. This would have created English, Irish, Scots and Welsh parliaments with powers over domestic issues but ultimately subordinate to the imperial Parliament in Westminster. This removed the anomaly in the Gladstonian solution referred to above.

Churchill came up with a third alternative. He did not believe that imperial affairs could in practice be separated from English party politics, which would create tension between the English assembly and the imperial Parliament. Instead, there should be a federalised solution with the UK divided into ten areas, each with a local administration and an elected assembly, conceding the vote to women with the right to serve on both bodies (an interesting concession as Churchill was regarded by suffragettes as an enemy of female emancipation). However, this radical solution, as Addison notes, would have turned the UK into a US or Canadian-style federation and was too radical for its day. So was a final variant put forward by Lloyd George suggesting that Ireland be conceded a limited form of Home Rule, while grand committees were set up at Westminster for England, Wales and Scotland.

But like most Liberals (and Englishmen), Churchill underestimated the passions the issue aroused across the Irish Sea. An Ulster Protestant MP once threw a book at him in the Commons which grazed his head, and during a visit to Belfast in 1912 he was howled down by a Unionist mob when he courageously, but perhaps unwisely, proclaimed that 'the flame of Irish nationality is inextinguishable'. Although he said that the pro-Ulster activities of the new Tory leader Bonar Law were 'almost treasonable' (some might delete the 'almost'), Churchill was in reality a compromiser on the Home Rule issue. The theme of consensus and the 'middle way', so prominent in Churchill's thinking throughout his political career, reasserted itself. In 1910 both he and Lloyd George had unsuccessfully tried to reach an agreement with the Tories on Ulster, and they continued to do so.

HOME SECRETARY

Churchill was appointed Home Secretary in 1911 and there were achievements here also, although some of his more eccentric tendencies were also on view. Paul Addison's book *Churchill on the Home Front* aptly includes a chapter heading 'Two Faces of a Home Secretary'. One face was the reformist face which had been shown to advantage at the Board of Trade. Churchill was appalled by the use of 'preventive detention' under the .1908 Prevention of Crimes Act which allowed punitive sentences of up to ten years to be added to sentences served by habitual offenders regardless of the triviality of the offences concerned (in one instance, only two shillings had been stolen), and discouraged its use. He was also zealous in reviewing sentences, often cutting them and although a firm supporter of hanging, he reprieved 49 per cent of those condemned to death during his period at the Home Office.

Less attractive was the paternalist face of Churchill as Home Secretary. He believed that tramps and wastrels should be sent to labour colonies, although these were never established. And like many at the time he was persuaded by the ideas of the eugenists who believed that the British race might be threatened by the 'unfit'. One answer was sterilisation, and Churchill did show some interest in the subject. Like many of his contemporaries he believed that 'weakness is definitely traceable in a great number of cases to parentage'. But before getting overexcited about these long-known facts (as Andrew Roberts does in his recent book *Eminent Churchillians*) it needs to be remembered that the Webbs, leading members of the progressive Labour Fabian Society, also believed in penal colonies for vagrants.

A third familiar face which Paul Addison might have added was Churchill the adventurer. For, in a freakish episode in Sidney Street in the East End of London, Churchill was alleged to have supervised personally the siege of a gang of anarchists. Martin Gilbert has knocked this myth firmly on the head in his biography, saying: 'At no point did Churchill direct the siege.' But he was in Sidney Street as a spectator, and contemporaries regarded this as reckless behaviour – adding to legends about the Home Secretary's need to be the centre of attention. The Tories mocked Churchill in the Commons.

More serious were accusations about Churchill's propensity for using force in strike situations. In Britain the period 1910–14 was notable for violent industrial episodes and some of them coincided with Churchill's term as Home Secretary. As late as 1950 in a general election campaign, Churchill was forced to deny the well-established myth in South Wales that he had sent troops to crush striking miners in Tonypandy. In fact he had not, and the trade union leader Ben Tillett paid tribute to his moderate role in the prolonged Dock Strike of 1911. But shortly after the almost farcical Sidney Street episode, Churchill was shown in an altogether less favourable light, and one which raised all the old doubts about his egotism and lack of judgement.

When a railway strike threatened to paralyse the country in 1911, Churchill set aside the normal provision that in the event of clashes with strikers (blackleg non-strike labour was hired by the railway companies) troops would only be called on if the civilian authorities requested them.

He mobilised some 50,000 troops without waiting for requests from local authorities and sent them to strategic points. Early on in the conflict, two strikers were shot dead by members of the Worcestershire regiment at Llanelli after they had tried to halt a train driven by blacklegs. Churchill was blamed by radical Liberals and members of the Labour Party. Any credit he had obtained from his sensitive handling of the Dock Strike was largely lost.

Why did Churchill act in this erratic way? Lloyd George, who took a more moderate view of the strike and eventually settled it in his role as Chancellor of the Exchequer, described him at the time as like 'a chauffeur who apparently is perfectly sane and drives with great skill for months, then suddenly takes you over a precipice'. Rhodes James suggests that Churchill's behaviour can be explained by his love of dramatic situations and 'lack of proportion', but Addison's more detailed study provides a more interesting explanation. Churchill, he claims, was worried about German subversion (in the same year, the Official Secrets Act was passed after a wave of hysteria about German spies – it remains on the statute books) and convinced himself that one Bebel, a German agent, had been bribing leaders of the railway unions. Other Cabinet members, according to the clerk of the Privy Council, regarded this as 'midsummer madness' although (Lloyd George apart) they supported Churchill's tough line against the strikers.

Just how tough this line was is reinforced by Churchill's quoted remark on the telephone to the Chancellor of the Exchequer when he heard that the strike had been settled. 'It would have been better to have gone on and given those men a good thrashing.' This sort of punitive nonsense displayed Churchill at his worst and, as Addison emphasises, was characteristic of the paternalist challenged. 'When sections of the working class began to challenge the state's authority, Churchill adopted a belligerent posture: the spirit of insubordination must be broken.' The Liberal reformer, Charles Masterman, whose friendship Churchill lost over the handling of the railway strike, described his condescending attitude to the lower classes as a desire for 'a state of things where a benign upper class dispensed benefits to an industrious . . . and grateful working class'. Later the Labour MP and historian Michael Foot would write that Churchill 'never had the foggiest notion of how the British people lived'. In this he was wrong. Churchill knew well enough how the people lived. But he wanted them to know their place. His appointment as Home Secretary marked a watershed in his political career for by the end of 1911 his phase as a radical reformer was over.

MARRIAGE

The hustle and bustle of Winston Churchill's political life left little time for romance. He confessed himself to be inept in his dealings with the opposite sex, writing to his future wife Clementine, 'I am stupid and clumsy in that relation, and naturally quite self-reliant and self-contained. By that path, I managed to arrive at loneliness.' There was a complication when Churchill's future sister-in-law Lady Gwendolyn Churchill ('Goonie' to the family) embarrassed the family by falling in love with him. Winston saved the situation by fleeing to Africa until she had recovered her senses. Otherwise Churchill's experience with women was limited, and when he first met Clementine Hozier, the daughter of a friend of Lady Churchill, he amazed her by standing and staring when she was expecting to be asked to dance! After this unpromising start, and despite two broken-off engagements for Clementine, the couple married in 1908.

'Clemmie,' as Winston called her, came from a well-known Liberal family but her father had died from alcoholism and her childhood had been a very difficult one. Although Prime Minister Asquith found Clemmie 'a thundering bore', it is clear that she did have some influences over her husband and could be a moderating influence on him in his dealings with his colleagues and subordinates.

Winston was never an easy husband for Clemmie. According to one biographer, she could be 'jealous and prickly' but this was not surprising given the multiplicity of Churchill's interests and the vastness of his ego. This in turn may have accounted for the seeming lack of interest which Clemmie showed in her children. Her work was cut out dealing with a dominant husband who also wanted from her the sort of love and affection he had only previously received from Mrs Everest. There is something both endearing and pathetic about Winston Churchill's letters to Clementine, addressing her as 'Mrs Kat' and signed 'Mr Pug' or 'Your Pig – lonely but fat' (often with a small pig drawn underneath).

The Churchills had four children. The three eldest – Diana, Randolph and Sarah – had turbulent and unhappy lives in the shadow of their famous father, even though he was often an indulgent and concerned parent. Only Mary, the youngest, achieved the sort of personal happiness that Churchill wanted and never quite achieved with Clementine.

timeline		
1904	Churchill leaves Tory Party
1906	Landslide Liberal election victory
1908	Churchill at Board of Trade. Marries Clementine Hozier
1909	Lloyd George's 'People's Budget' introduced
1910	Appointed Home Secretary. Twin elections destroy Liberal majority
1911	Parliament Act passed.

4

THE WARRIOR

FIRST LORD OF THE ADMIRALTY

In October 1911, Winston Churchill replaced Reginald McKenna as First Lord of the Admiralty while McKenna took his post as Home Secretary. Strictly speaking this was a demotion because the post of Home Secretary (together with those of Foreign Secretary and Chancellor) was one of the three senior posts in the government. However, Churchill had long wanted an opportunity to control one of the service ministries. He was, says one biographer, 'happier than he had ever been' at the prospect of running the Royal Navy. His romantic belief in military glory and prowess was stirred by the knowledge that he would be the master of the navy's battleships, those 'war castles foaming to their stations'.

Churchill took over the Admiralty at an important moment. Earlier in that same year the British government had stood by its French ally in the so-called Agadir Crisis, when the Germans had interfered in Morocco which, at that point, was deemed to be in the French sphere of influence in North Africa. Lloyd George had made a belligerent speech at the Mansion House in London effectively warning the Germans off, and Churchill had strongly supported him. The need for Britain to preserve its naval superiority in the face of an expanding German programme of naval building seemed clear to Churchill. The fact that only three years earlier he had criticized the size of the naval budget characteristically did not worry him.

Despite his previous record, Churchill proved to be an innovatory First Lord of the Admiralty. He introduced fifteen-inch guns on battleships, and replaced obsolete, coal-burning ships with new, oil-fired vessels. But he also enjoyed the perks of the Admiralty the lavish entertaining and especially the use of the Admiralty yacht *Enchantress* with its 100 sailors and 4000 ton displacement. This caused resentment elsewhere and the press were especially critical of Churchill's use of the yacht to entertain friends and family. But Churchill didn't care about such minor issues. Solemnly he warned against the expanding German fleet which was at the disposal of a 'military and bureaucratic oligarchy supported by a powerful Junker landlord class'. Yet at the same time he pressed the Germans in 1913 for a 'naval holiday' which, he pointed out, would save them up to seven million pounds if their plan to build three more dreadnought battleships in that year was dropped. The Germans rejected these overtures and so in May 1913, Churchill steered his own naval law through the House of Commons which provided the Royal Navy with five more battleships.

It is easy to see Churchill's tenure at the Admiralty as a natural progression for the young man who had so gloried in his military feats in the Sudan and on the north-west frontier of India. But this is almost certainly to oversimplify a complex personality. For as Paul Addison points out, the paternalist streak which he had shown at the Board of Trade and the Home Office, though now overriden by defence priorities, had not altogether disappeared. Churchill secured, for example, a pay rise for the able seamen (the first since 1857), and was also active in attempting to improve their on-shore accommodation and leisure facilities. Typically though, his egocentricity offended admirals and officers alike and he was accused of arrogance and conceit. He may, as the *Daily Express* recorded, have been 'Here, There, and Everywhere', but this presence was not always welcome.

Nevertheless Churchill was able, by a blend of progressive thinking and raising of traditional bogeys, to secure what he wanted from his Cabinet colleagues for the navy. Failure to raise sailors' pay, he pointed out, might have dire consequences at a time (in 1912) when there was widespread industrial discontent in the country. Dissatisfied mariners, he noted, could be stirred up to mutiny by German agents (an echo of the 1911 rail strike) and 'We have had great mutinies in the past in the British Navy.' If the German bogey didn't work, Churchill was not above a little horse-trading. In 1913 he secured Lloyd George's support for increased naval expenditure by promising support for the Chancellor's pet land reform scheme which proposed to look at rates, rents and agricultural workers' wages.

Despite this pragmatism, however, it was clear to Churchill's contemporaries that the radical reformer of 1908 had become a supporter of national military power by 1912. By 1913–14 his excessive campaigning for increased naval spending had made him unpopular with rank-and-file Liberals. And this, together with his attempts to find common ground with the Ulster Unionists, made him suspect as a reliable party member, the same condemnation that was thrown at him by Tories before 1904. His Cabinet colleagues Simon, Runciman and Samuel became so angered by his deviations from official Liberal policy that they tried unsuccessfully to secure his resignation.

THE OUTBREAK OF WAR

Like almost all his contemporaries, Churchill did not foresee the outbreak of war in July 1914. At the time, the Asquith Liberal government was mainly concerned about the possibility of civil war in Ireland over the issue of Home Rule. (Extensive gun-running and civil disobedience by Ulster Protestants made this seem a real possibility before the Nationalist leader Redmond generously put the question into abeyance for the duration of the war.)

At the outset it did not seem that the assassination of the heir to the Austro-Hungarian throne Franz Ferdinand by a Bosnian Serb in Sarajevo was of any great concern to Britain. Churchill himself said at the time, 'Balkan quarrels are no concern of ours.' But by 27 July, the day after the conciliatory Serb reply to an aggressive Austrian ultimatum accusing Serbia of complicity in the murder, Churchill was concerned enough to order the First Fleet at Portland 'not to disperse for manoeuvre for the present'. He was to write later that the Liberal government hoped that the German Emperor William II 'would understand' this innocent precaution. However, Churchill was personally convinced that the Royal Navy could master the German High Seas fleet in any coming war. 'I feel sure,' he wrote to Clemmie, 'that if war came we shall give them a good drubbing.' In the meantime he ordered oil tanks and ammunition depots to be guarded.

Germany was an ally of Austria-Hungary just as Russia was of Serbia, and the German attitude in the crisis was crucial. France too would become involved if Germany attacked its ally Russia. At this stage, a majority of the British Cabinet, including Churchill, did not want to go to war if Germany attacked France. This was despite the fact that

Churchill himself had negotiated a naval agreement in 1912 leaving control of the Mediterranean to the French fleet, and allowing the Royal Navy to concentrate its strength in the North Sea. But he and his colleagues could not know that the German Schlieffen Plan predetermined their response to a war between Russia and Austria-Hungary in which Germany felt bound to side with Austria-Hungary. The Schlieffen Plan provided that Germany would attack Russia's ally France through neutral Belgium, so breaking the 1839 treaty under whose terms both Britain, France and Germany (or Prussia as it then was) were guarantors of the country's neutrality. Before Belgium's neutrality was threatened, Churchill had felt that as no treaty obligation bound Britain to fight with France, she should stay out of the conflict, as did most of his colleagues.

BRITAIN DECLARES WAR

All this changed when Germany invaded Belgium in August 1914, although Lloyd George was reluctant to see Britain involved in a war until the last moment (two other Liberal cabinet ministers resigned). Churchill, by contrast, threw himself into the war effort after the declaration of war on Germany with an enthusiasm which sometimes unnerved colleagues. 'Winston has got on his war paint,' noted Asquith, while Lloyd George remarked that 'You could see he was a really happy man.'

The historian David Reynolds has written that in 1914 Britain 'had a vast navy that was irrelevant to continental land war, and an army with a continental strategy but no means of making an impact'. This was largely true. Not until 1916 did Britain have an army in France which could match those of the French and Germans in numerical terms, and once the British Expeditionary Force was safely transported to France in 1914, the Royal Navy's superiority was irrelevant to the bloody slogging match which started on the Western Front.

ANTWERP

However, Churchill, as always, was itching for action. He busied himself by devising schemes to embarrass the Germans but his first major intervention in the First World War was in a defensive mode. This was because the rapid German advance through Belgium soon endangered the great port of Antwerp, and Churchill became personally involved in its defence. But it was his Cabinet colleagues rather than the Germans who were most embarrassed by a melodramatic offer to resign his post and take command of the defence of Antwerp in person. Churchill added the proviso that he be 'given necessary military rank and authority, and full powers of a commander of a detached force in the field'. Asquith rejected the request and Antwerp fell anyway, but Churchill subsequently claimed in his book *The World Crisis* that 'ten days were won' which delayed the German advance and allowed the Allies to cling on to the tiny strip of land around Ypres. The military historian Sir Michael Howard is inclined to accept Churchill's defence of his involvement, but at the time, the opposition press was savage. Here was Churchill going off on reckless adventures while the Germans sank merchant ships in the South Atlantic and bombarded coastal towns like Scarborough and Whitby.

GALLIPOLI AND DISGRACE

Antwerp was in fact the prelude to an even worse disaster for Churchill. Ironically it came from the correct perception by Churchill, Lloyd George and others that the Western Front was little more than a slaughter-house which, contrary to predictions that the war would 'be over by Christmas', showed no signs in 1915 of providing the Allies with a decisive victory. Instead, as Churchill remarked, British troops were being sent 'to chew barbed wire in Flanders'.

The alternative strategy put forward by Churchill and the so-called 'Easterners' was to knock out the Dardanelles forts, land Allied troops in Gallipoli, drive Turkey out of the war (she had entered it on the German side in 1914), and spark off a revolt in the Balkans against Austria-Hungary. Most importantly, a successful landing would open up a new supply route through the Black Sea to Britain's ally, Russia, which was hamstrung by a shortage of munitions (although, as Norman Stone has pointed out in his seminal book on the Eastern Front, such shortages were not as drastic as has sometimes been suggested). There is no doubt that Churchill was the leading advocate of this operation within the

British government. But he had the support and approval of Prime Minister Asquith and the Secretary of State for War, Kitchener, who had an almost godlike status as the victor of the Sudanese and South African wars.

It is arguable that the operation to seize the forts, preceded by a naval bombardment, was fatally flawed from the start. For in October 1914 Churchill himself had ordered a bombardment of the Dardanelles forts in a revenge attack for the cover supplied by use of the Turkish flag for the German commerce raiders *Goeben* and *Breslau*. The naval historian Arthur Marder has concluded that 'The cost of this premature attack far outweighed the slight advantages, since it put the Turks and their German military advisers on the alert.' Subsequently Churchill bore a good deal of responsibility for insisting that the forcing of the Dardanelles should be 'a purely naval operation' against the advice of the admiral on the spot who wanted the army to be involved. En route, Churchill lost the support of the First Sea Lord Jackie Fisher (thought to be deranged at the time, he later went mad) and by the autumn of 1915, it became clear that the operation had failed after landings had been attempted and bloodily repulsed.

If Churchill was to blame, that blame in the view of most historians was only partial. But at the time, the verdict was savage, most bitterly put perhaps by the Australian Monash (Gallipoli was a particular disaster for the Australian army) who said that the fiasco was a result of 'the Churchill way of rushing in before we are ready, and hardly knowing what you are going to do next'.

For Churchill personally, the Gallipoli disaster was a case of chickens coming home to roost. He had antagonised senior naval officers and Cabinet colleagues alike by his behaviour during his entire period at the Admiralty since 1911. The Commander-in-Chief Jellicoe said that Churchill was 'a public menace to the British Empire' and Asquith, who had often protected him from critics before, found him 'intolerable, noisy, long-winded and full of perorations'. Churchill subsequently admitted that he had got 'a bit above himself' at the Admiralty but he had no real conception of how unpopular he had become (the Tories, of course, loathed him and, as outlined before, many rank-and-file Liberals also regarded him with suspicion). When, belatedly he did, Churchill wrote a grovelling letter to Asquith saying he would serve in the Government in any capacity whatever. This suited Asquith. After much pressure the Prime Minister finally formed a coalition government in May 1915 when there were already signs that the Gallipoli operation was in trouble. The price of Tory support was that Churchill be demoted to a minor post, and Asquith pushed him into the sinecure post of Chancellor of the Duchy of Lancaster which was outside the Cabinet. The total failure of Gallipoli allowed the Tories to demand the head of the most hated member of the Liberal Party. They got it when Winston Churchill resigned from the government altogether in November 1915.

Exile from government was a devastating blow and his wife believed for a time that Churchill 'would die of grief'. Yet in January 1916, he obtained a commission as Commander of the Sixth Battalion Royal Scots Fusiliers with the rank of captain. The wheel had turned full circle for the man who started his career as a fledgling second lieutenant from Sandhurst.

FRONTLINE SOLDIER

After accepting his commission in the Royal Scots Fusiliers, Churchill served for 100 days near Ploegstreet in Flanders. Even at this distance, however, what Addison calls 'the high fever of politics' remained with him. Churchill campaigned for the introduction of conscription in Britain as he had done while still in office. When Asquith resisted the suggestion, he urged Lloyd George to resign over the issue. But he remained a political leper. When Asquith was replaced as Prime Minister by Lloyd George in December 1916, Churchill received no offer of a government job, primarily because he was still anathema to the Tory Party. Lloyd George had wanted to re-employ his old ally, but the new dominant position of the Conservatives in the Coalition wouldn't allow this. The Liberal Party had split over the appointment of Lloyd George, with part of the party siding with Asquith and refusing to back the new Coalition.

Gradually though, Captain Churchill, who was well enough liked by his soldiers at the Front (one of whom was to recall that the disgraced politician had 'accelerated the morale of officers and men to an almost unbelievable degree'), began a slow return to the political arena. In March 1917, the Report on the Dardanelles Commission partly exonerated him from responsibility for the disaster, and by July 1917, Lloyd George felt sufficiently reassured to appoint him Minister of Munitions. Lloyd George had not, however, consulted the Tories about this appointment, and there was a violent protest so that, in Martin Gilbert's words, the life of the Coalition Government 'trembled in the balance'. Here was another reminder to Churchill of the depth of unpopularity he had achieved in his old party.

Churchill had completed his last period of active military service, but he retained his interest in all things military and with it, the whiff of accusation that he was a reckless adventurer who would, if given a chance, bring about another Gallipoli bloodbath.

timeline	1911		Agadir Crisis.
			Churchill becomes First Lord of the Admiralty
	1913		Churchill suggests 'naval holiday'
	1914		Outbreak of the First World War
	1915		Gallipoli campaign.
		May	Coalition Government formed.
		November	Churchill resigns from Government
	1916		Churchill obtains commission in Scots Guards.
			Battle of the Somme
		December	Lloyd George becomes Prime Minister.
	1917 July		Churchill returns to Government as Minister of Munitions

Points to consider

1) **Assess Churchill's role in the determining of British naval strategy before 1914.**
2) **To what extent was Churchill to blame for the failure of the Gallipoli Campaign?**

5

THE RETURN OF A RENEGADE

CHURCHILL AND LLOYD GEORGE

Between 1917 and 1922 Churchill found himself back in partnership with his old Liberal Party mentor David Lloyd George. There is no doubt that Churchill felt betrayed by Lloyd George at the time of the Gallipoli failure, and Clementine felt even more strongly that the Welshman was the 'direct descendant of Judas Iscariot'. But Churchill knew that he would have to work with the dynamic Prime Minister and, according to Lloyd George's biographer John Grigg, the two men were 'on excellent terms' in the closing stages of the Great War. Churchill was busy with preparations to amass enough munitions to take the war into 1920, and his growing drift to the right was emphasised when he tried unsuccessfully to deprive striking workers in tank factories of their exemption from military service. Even the Tory leader Bonar Law had opposed such a move.

Under Lloyd George, Churchill was to take on the double load of the Air Ministry and the War Office after the so-called 'khaki election' of December 1918 which had given the Coalition an overwhelming majority over Labour and the rump of the Liberal Party under Asquith.

Did Churchill feel dwarfed by his new association with the 'man who won the war', who had also been very much the senior partner in the pre-war Liberal Government? One anecdote told by his parliamentary Private Secretary suggests that he did. It concerned a meeting in 1924 when Lloyd George, unlike Churchill, was out of office. When asked about the conversation Churchill allegedly replied, 'Within five minutes the old relationship was completely re-established. The relationship between Master and Servant. And I was the servant.' However, Grigg doubts whether this version of events holds up. Churchill, in his view, was unlikely to be in awe of any man.

Churchill, Secretary of State for War, in Cologne, August 1919

RUSSIA AND THE BOLSHEVIKS

By the autumn of 1918, it was becoming clear that the Allies would win the war. The last great German offensives in France had failed in the spring of 1918, and Germany's allies were starting to collapse. There was, Churchill noted on hearing of Austria-Hungary's surrender in October, 'a drizzle of empires falling through the air'. When the Germans did eventually ask for an armistice, which came into effect on 11 November 1918, Churchill supported Lloyd George's demands for moderate treatment of Germany. But the feeling of the time was against him and there was an atmosphere of anti-German hysteria in the 'khaki election' of December 1918. A reference to a 'moderate peace' in a speech made by Churchill to his constituents was drowned by hecklers.

By this time in any case, it was Russia, not Germany, that was uppermost in Churchill's thoughts. On 10 November, the day before the German armistice, Churchill had warned his Cabinet colleagues about the new Bolshevik government which had just come to power there. The

Bolsheviks, said Churchill in his usual florid style, were 'ferocious baboons' and it was therefore 'important to get Germany on her legs again for fear of the spread of Bolshevism'. For some time to come, while Lloyd George was deeply involved in the evolution of the peace settlement with Germany, Churchill was obsessed with the Russian problem, and insistent that the Bolsheviks be over-thrown. Lloyd George, although equally hostile to the Bolshevik ideas of international revolution, was more pragmatic. The conquest of Russia, he pointed out tartly, would cost hundreds of millions of pounds and require an army of half a million men. Neither would be forthcoming and the trade unions and Labour had started a 'hands off Russia' campaign. Churchill's 'vain fretting' about Russia, said his political overlord, was a waste of his energies which would be better deployed elsewhere. Lloyd George won the argument but Churchill did not change his opinions. In his eyes, 'the Bolshevik tyranny' was 'the worst, the most destructive, the most degrading' in world history.

A cartoon by David Low, published in the Evening Standard *(1920). It was entitled:* Winston's bag. He hunts lions and brings home decayed cats.

IRELAND

At the end of 1920 Lloyd George moved Churchill to the Colonial Office where he had started his governmental career. There he remained until the fall of the Lloyd George Coalition in October 1922. But the Prime Minister was still keen to use Churchill's experience in other spheres, and he played a key role in the 'settlement' of the Irish problem in 1921. The massive Sinn Fein victory in the 1918 general election had not persuaded the Unionists to change their views about Home Rule, but it did initiate a war of independence against the British in the 26 Nationalist counties. Churchill strongly supported the punitive measures Lloyd George took against the Irish Republican Army, although these tended to rebound on the Irish civilian population (the centre of Cork being burnt down by the notorious British irregulars known as the 'Black and Tans', for example). Lloyd George boasted that 'we have murder by the throat' but by 1920 both sides were exhausted by the struggle, and ready for a settlement. This duly came in the shape of the 1921 Anglo-Irish Treaty which conceded independence within the British Empire and Commonwealth, to the 26 counties of the south under the name of the Irish Free State.

Churchill assisted the settlement by establishing a good working relationship with Michael Collins, the former head of the IRA, whom he subsequently encouraged to crush the anti-treaty faction of that organisation in the Irish civil war of 1922–3 (which cost Collins his own life). He was also entrusted by Lloyd George with the task of steering the Act which acknowledged the independence of the Free State through the House of Commons, even though he was not the Chief Secretary for Ireland. This, notes Martin Gilbert, was an acknowledgement by his old ally of 'Churchill's skills both as a conciliator and a master of detailed exposition'. His speech to the House, stressing the fact that the Free State would remain inside the Empire and that Britain would still have the use of the so-called 'treaty-ports' had, according to Austen Chamberlain, 'a profound effect' on it.

THE FALL OF THE COALITION

Lloyd George, meanwhile, had become embroiled in a serious Near Eastern crisis by backing Greece in its efforts to secure territory in Asia

Minor. The so-called 'Chanak Crisis' showed that for once the adroit Welshman had backed the wrong horse as it was the Turks under Kemal Ataturk who emerged triumphant. Churchill, initially cautious about taking a strong line against Turkey (the defeated ally of Germany in the First World War), eventually gave full support to the Prime Minister but Lloyd George's political reputation was fatally damaged. A famous meeting of Tory backbenchers at the Carlton Club in October 1922 made it clear that their party would support Lloyd George no longer. Chanak proved to be Lloyd George's Gallipoli, but for him, unlike Churchill, there was to be no recovery. Never again was this most influential of politicians to hold political office.

For Churchill, the fall of the Lloyd George Coalition was also to mean his temporary exclusion from the House of Commons, the central focus for his life. In the 1922 general election which followed Lloyd George's resignation, Churchill lost his seat in Dundee although this defeat, as Addison notes, in a 'poor and depressed industrial constituency' was not entirely his fault. Churchill himself said, 'When one thinks of the kind of lives the poorer people of Dundee have to live one cannot be indignant at the way they voted' (a statement which effectively refutes Michael Foot's remark, quoted earlier, that Churchill had no conception of how most British people lived).

RETURN OF A RENEGADE

Winston Churchill had left the Tory Party in 1904 and held Cabinet office as a Liberal for 15 years. For many Conservatives during that period, he had been the most hated man in the rival party, the more so because he was regarded as a political turncoat. But from 1911 onwards, there had been a perceptible rightwards shift in Churchill's views which coincided with the rise of Labour and the decline of Liberalism. Forced out of his parliamentary seat in 1922, he spent six months pondering over both his future and his political allegiance. During this time Churchill told a leading Conservative that he was 'a Tory Democrat', but for him the key issue was still free trade. So when Stanley Baldwin, who had replaced Bonar Law as the Tory leader, announced his conversion to tariff protection, Churchill still felt obliged to throw in his lot with the Liberals. Nevertheless his constant references to 'the socialist menace' in his campaign for the West Leicester seat in the general election of December 1923 showed that fighting the left was rapidly becoming his political priority.

Churchill lost but so did Stanley Baldwin and the Tories just as they did in 1906 when Chamberlain had converted the Party to protectionism. Had they won, some historians have suggested, Churchill might well have resumed his old alliance with Lloyd George on an anti-protection ticket. As it was, the temporary reconciliation between Lloyd George and the Asquithian Liberals proved to be short-lived, and did not halt the long-term political decline of the Liberal Party.

In fact, the 1923 general election produced Britain's first Labour government under Ramsay MacDonald. A temporary reconciliation between the Liberals of both Lloyd George and Asquithian varieties had been effected in order to put Labour in and so prevent the Tories, with the largest popular vote, taking office again.

Party	Votes	Seats	% vote
Conservatives	5,538,824	258	38.1
Liberals	4,311,147	159	29.6
Labour	4,438,508	191	30.5
Others	260,042	7	1.8
Electorate: 21,281,232		Percentage turnout: 70.8	

Table 1: 1923 election result

Churchill strongly opposed this decision. Here was the 'socialist menace' in the halls and corridors of Whitehall – although Labour's subsequent behaviour in office did little to justify this high-blown rhetoric. But it was probably this decision by his old Liberal colleagues in the House of Commons that made Churchill finally decide to switch his support back to the Tories because they, in Paul Addison's words, were 'the natural party of resistance to Socialism'.

The Tories were glad to have him. Under Baldwin, the Conservatives lacked political leaders of serious weight because the Party had long been excluded from office and Churchill, whatever his reputation, had years of mature experience in government to offer. For his part, Churchill seemed to realise that to become acceptable to Baldwin, a 'one nation' Tory anxious to prevent class antagonism, a softer tone on social

Party	Votes	Seats	% vote
Conservatives	8,039,598	419	48.3
Liberals	2,928,747	40	17.6
Labour	5,489,077	151	33.0
Communists	55,346	1	0.3
Others	126,511		
Electorate: 21,731,320		Percentage turnout: 76.6	

Table 2: 1924 election result

policy was needed. Standing as an Independent in the Abbey Division of Westminster in the March 1924 by-election, Churchill reminded his audience that 'I have a number of measures of social reform to my credit. These seem to have been forgotten.'

Churchill lost again, but he drifted inevitably towards reunion with the Conservatives. In May 1924, he spoke to a Conservative Party Association for the first time in 20 years, and Tory Central Office then agreed to support him under the label of 'Constitutionalist' in Epping (a title used when candidates were anti-Labour and the Liberals and Tories had agreed to co-operate against Labour. There was no such pact in Epping in fact, but Churchill was trying to secure Liberal support). Epping was to be Churchill's last parliamentary constituency; he continued to represent it until 1964.

The general election of October 1924 was fought in an atmosphere of anti-socialist hysteria because of the 'Zinoviev letter', a probable forgery which appeared to indicate that Communists were plotting a revolution in Britain and affected the Labour vote. This helped Churchill to win easily in Epping with a majority of 9000 votes, and the Tories came back into office with a substantial majority. Churchill was now, to all intents and purposes, a Conservative once again. But what was the Tory leadership going to do with this renegade?

CHANCELLOR

Many Conservatives still regarded Churchill with fear and suspicion. But Baldwin thought it better to have Churchill inside the government where he would be bound by loyalty to his colleagues than outside it like a rogue elephant on the back-benches. The problem facing the inexperienced Prime Minister was where to put his new recruit. The scene was dramatic. Churchill was summoned to see Baldwin in Downing Street. Would he, Baldwin asked, be prepared to take on the post of Chancellor of the Exchequer? Churchill wrote later:

> I should have liked to have answered, 'Will the bloody duck swim?', but as it was a formal and important conversation I replied, 'This fulfils my ambition. I still have my father's robes as Chancellor. I shall be proud to serve you in this splendid office.'

As always, the ghost of Lord Randolph hovered over his son.

There is little doubt that Churchill was surprised by Baldwin's offer of the third greatest public office in Britain. Should historians be so, however? According to Baldwin's biographer Roy Jenkins, the 'extraordinary suggestion' was Neville Chamberlain's idea (he had been Chancellor in the short 1922–3 Tory administration) and Baldwin had 'jumped at the idea'. This, he alleges, is because Chamberlain believed that any government post for Churchill would provoke such 'a howl' in the Tory ranks that it didn't much matter whether he were given the Exchequer or a more junior post such as the Admiralty. By contrast, Chamberlain's own biographer David Dilks states that Baldwin (advised by Neville's half-brother Austen) offered the post to Chamberlain first in the expectation that he (wishing to become Health Minister) would reject it. Chamberlain did not think he would be a good Chancellor (though ironically he was to hold this post continuously from 1932 to 1937), but he believed he would be a good Health Minister. Only when Chamberlain had refused the post did Baldwin offer it to Churchill.

Charmley, by contrast, in his biography says Baldwin was trying to win over former Liberals to the Tories. If this was Baldwin's strategy, it was not a very successful one as the two rival wings of the Liberal Party continued to exist under Lloyd George and Asquith even if their combined vote continued to collapse (despite a temporary resurgence in the 1929 election). Yet Churchill himself recognised the significance of Baldwin's appointment. 'You have done more for me than Lloyd George ever did' – a telling point as Baldwin's antipathy to the former Prime Minister was well known. Arguably, Churchill had returned to his natural home.

timeline	1918 November	Armistice ending the First World War
	December	Lloyd George Coalition wins 'khaki election'
	1918-21	Allied intervention in Russia
	1921	Anglo-Irish Treaty steered through Commons by Churchill
	1922 October	Fall of Lloyd George Coalition. Churchill loses seat in Dundee
	1924 November	First Labour government under MacDonald. Tories win general election. Churchill appointed Chancellor of the Exchequer by Baldwin

Points to Consider

1) **Account for Winston Churchill's return to the Tory Party by 1924.**
2) **What role did Churchill play in the major policy decisions of the Lloyd George Coalition between 1918 and 1922?**

6

TORY CHANCELLOR

If he was at home in most respects in Baldwin's Tory Party, Churchill remained an unrepentant free trader. In this sense his appointment to the Treasury was a victory for free trade because Baldwin had abandoned the tariff policy which had brought about the defeat of the Conservatives in the 1923 general election.

THE DECISION TO RETURN TO THE GOLD STANDARD

The economy of the pre-1914 world was based on a system whereby most leading currencies were convertible into fixed values of gold. The pound sterling had a fixed value against gold and could be exchanged at the rate of one pound for $4.86.

Economists at that time believed that if a nation went into deficit on its balance of trade account, it would begin to lose its gold reserves and would be forced to put up interest rates (fixed by the Bank of England's judgement on the correct rate of interest for its loans to the joint stock banks) to attract an inflow of more gold. Prices would then fall, exports would become more competitive, and a balance of trade surplus, with the value of exports exceeding imports, would be restored. This was the financial orthodoxy in the world in which the youthful Winston Churchill grew up. He believed that it was closely linked to the free trade system which was based on the laws of supply and demand in international trade which did not require government intervention. The historian Peter Clarke has pointed out that Churchill held these beliefs strongly between 1900, when he first entered the Commons, and 1930.

He was not shifted from these beliefs by the Government decision in 1919 to abandon the $4.86 parity with the dollar, when roaring inflation made it impossible to sustain. In March 1919, the British Government suspended Britain's attachment to the Gold Standard and allowed the pound to float and find its own value on the exchange markets. By the beginning of 1920, the value of sterling against the US dollar had fallen from $4.86, the pre-war rate, to $3.40.

It remained the policy of the Treasury, however, to return to the Gold Standard in the long run, and by 1925 deflationary policies had pushed the exchange rate value of the pound up to $4.63. (It should be noted that the Labour Party also supported the return to the Gold Standard.) When Churchill took office in 1924, he was also operating under another constraint because the 1920 Act which had discontinued the relationship with the Gold Standard in Britain, was due to be suspended on 31 December 1925. Churchill seemed, initially at any rate, to have few doubts about the desirability of restoring the Gold Standard or the ease with which this goal could be achieved. Indeed, he told Baldwin in 1925 that 'It will be easy to attain the Gold Standard.'

But as the moment grew nearer Churchill began to have doubts. Unemployment had remained consistently high in Britain since the end of the Great War, and Churchill feared that restoration of the Gold Standard would push the Bank Rate up to five or six per cent which would represent 'a very serious check' to trade and industry and so push unemployment even higher. Addison points out that Churchill never received a satisfactory answer to this anxiety either from Montagu Norman, the Governor of the Bank of England, or from his Treasury advisers. It was for this reason that he invited John Maynard Keynes, the famous Cambridge economist and a known opponent of the return to the Gold Standard, to dinner at Number Eleven Downing Street, and circulated a paper to his Treasury officials putting the case against it.

Nevertheless, Churchill did make the decision to return to the Gold Standard at the end of 1925, with the consequences that the critics of this move had predicted. But Churchill's scepticism apparently showed that he acted only on the presumption that the Governor of the Bank of England and his Treasury colleagues were right, and that he, an amateur in economic matters, must take their advice. He therefore argued publicly that return to the Gold Standard would give the working-class wage stability and that if Britain did not return to it, the Dominions might go on the Gold Standard on their own, giving them an advantage in their trade with the United States. Finally, Churchill maintained that the Gold Standard was essential to maintain the value of the currency and prevent deflation. In reality, as Keynes had foreseen, the return to gold made British exports less competitive in world markets and precipitated the financial crisis of 1929-31 and even higher unemployment.

Churchill's Responsibility

In later years Churchill tried to distance himself from responsibility for the decision to return to the Gold Standard, especially as this decision was linked by his critics to the coming of the Depression after 1929. Churchill himself said in 1931 that something 'terrible is going to happen financially. I hope we shall hang Montagu Norman if it does. I will certainly turn King's evidence against him'. This scenario of the Gold Standard decision has the Governor of the Bank of England as the culprit. It was endorsed by Churchill a decade later when he told his personal physician Lord Moran that as Chancellor he had been seduced by the 'blandishments' of the Governor who persuaded him to return to gold and 'had then left him severely alone'. Particularly damning in retrospect was Norman's remark at the time that the domestic impact of 'dear money' (that being a result of raising the Bank Rate) was 'much more psychological than real'.

Do the facts bear out such an interpretation? Keynes certainly noted in his otherwise critical *The Economic Consequences of Mr Churchill* that 'he was gravely misled by his experts'. And even historians like Clive Ponting, generally severely critical of Churchill, accept that he harboured doubts about the Gold Standard decision.

But how real were these doubts? In his contribution to the definitive compilation of essays about Churchill, edited by Blake and Louis, Peter Clarke stresses the consistency of Churchill's economic thinking, and denies the suggestion that he was an economic ignoramus. On the contrary, Clarke points out that he was better prepared for the Chancellorship than Lloyd George, Baldwin (briefly Chancellor under Bonar Law in 1922) and Neville Chamberlain. Churchill, runs this argument, was a firm supporter of the Gladstonian principle of 'sound finance' and the virtues of free trade. He had held these beliefs since the start of his parliamentary career, and once in office as Chancellor he had, according to his Private Secretary, 'a great hankering to be considered orthodox'. As Chancellor, therefore, whatever his fears about long-term unemployment, Churchill clung to his old free trade principles and their link to the Gold Standard 'amid the shifting sands of his other vicissitudes'. They, says Clarke, 'formed a rock to which he clung'.

This particular rock proved to be too porous, and the 1929-31 crash destroyed Churchill's belief in orthodox finance which, Clarke argues, was a product in any case of his belief in the sanctity of the British Empire and the virtues of free trade. After 1930–31 Churchill ceased to be a free-trader, just as his party had abandoned the principle under Neville Chamberlain's stewardship at the Treasury.

If this thesis is correct there was nothing surprising about Churchill's decision to return to the Gold Standard in 1925, which can be seen as the inevitable consequence of his long-held belief in the principles of free trade and financial orthodoxy.

THE GENERAL STRIKE

The other great issue in which Churchill became involved during his Chancellorship was the General Strike of 1926. This arose from long-standing grievances in the National Union of Miners about wages and conditions which were not satisfied by the report of the government-sponsored Samuel Commission in 1926. Samuel endorsed the mine-owner's demand for a cut in wages, and rejected their demand that the Government should continue its subsidy to a coal industry which was being seriously affected by cheap foreign coal imports. But the Commission did agree with the miners about the maintenance of the seven-hour day and recommended nationalisation of mineral rights.

Churchill denounced nationalisation of mineral rights on the ground that 'one instalment of nationalisation would lead to another'. He had negotiated the principle of the eight-hour day as President of the Board of Trade and now wanted its restoration, but preparations for the 1926 Budget reduced his involvement in the protracted negotiations with the Trades Union Congress which supported the miners' claims, before the ten-day General Strike started in May 1926. It was Stanley Baldwin who conceived the Government's pre-strike strategy.

Churchill's attitude to the miners and their supporters in the trade union movement was belligerent. 'I am quite ready to fight with the coal miners,' he told his Private Secretary in a letter and when the industrial dispute was widened by the support of other unions into the General Strike, he pressed for the toughest of measures against the strikers.

The General Strike meant that Fleet Street printers were on strike. So, to put the Government's case Churchill was put in charge of *The British Gazette*, an emergency news-sheet which would allow him to use his journalistic talents and, according to Stanley Baldwin, stop him 'doing worse things' (Baldwin told his official biographer that 'he [Churchill] would have wanted to shoot someone' although a reference to this effect was deleted by G.M. Young after Churchill objected). Even so, *The British Gazette* showed Churchill's influence by making wild accusations about Bolshevik links with the strikers, provoking Lloyd George to remark that the paper was 'clothed in the tawdry garb of third-rate journalism'. His management style also provoked resentment amongst the journalists so that one Tory leader, pleading with Baldwin to rein in Churchill's excesses, remarked that 'he thinks he is Napoleon' – which was not so wide of the mark given Winston Churchill's known admiration for the French Emperor! Rhodes James' measured judgement on the role of *The British Gazette* seems a fair one. 'No one,' he wrote, 'has ever suggested that its influence was beneficial.'

Baldwin also appointed Churchill to the Supply and Transport Committee which was set up by the Government to organise an alternative system to replace the one closed down by the trade unions. He alarmed colleagues by his willingness to draft in the military at every turn, and his use of phrases like 'we are at war'. This was the Churchill of Sidney Street, charging about like 'a bull in a china shop' and fully justifying, it seemed, Baldwin's comment at the outset of the strike that he was 'terrified of what Winston was going to be like'.

Churchill also wanted the Government to take over full control of the newly-founded BBC, a demand which Baldwin correctly resisted for, as Sir John Reith, its first Director-General blandly admitted, the Government knew it could trust the Corporation 'not to be really impartial'.

Churchill's Role in Retrospect

Shortly after the end of the General Strike, when the TUC had left the miners to carry on their struggle alone, the left-wing journal *The New Statesman* accused Churchill and his great friend Birkenhead of being part of a 'war party' which forced Baldwin to break off negotiations with the TUC just as they were about to succeed. Similar accusations were made by the great trade unionist and later wartime colleague of Churchill, Ernest Bevin. It remained a myth of the Left for years, but only historians as consistently hostile to Churchill as Clive Ponting have given it any credence in recent years.

Addison points out that Churchill's preparations for the 1926 Budget kept him out of most of the late negotiations with the TUC and Rhodes James believed that it was 'unreasonable to select him specifically for condemnation'. He goes on to make the significant point that it was Churchill's behaviour *during* the General Strike that was responsible for the accusations that were subsequently made, stating that he had helped to precipitate it.

Churchill's behaviour during the General Strike is plainly another matter. Even Gilbert, Churchill's most sympathetic biographer concedes that he asked too much from the staff of *The British Gazette*. Addision also notes that whereas Baldwin merely wanted the strikers to 'admit they have done wrong', Churchwill wanted the strike broken by piling on the pressure. Baldwin's subtle tactic of trying to detach the TUC leadership from the miners was ultimately successful, for throughout, those men (Thomas, Citrine *et al*) showed less appetite for the industrial battle than the rank-and-file trade unionists.

In another sense, as Baldwin himself admitted, Churchill may have played into the Prime Minister's hands. It was convenient for Baldwin that the perception of Churchill as a rogue elephant during the General Strike should show him in an equivalently favourable light as the wise compromiser, anxious to dampen down class tensions.

Aftermath

Whether Baldwin really deserves this reputation is debatable. It was he after all who sanctioned the punitive 1927 Trades Disputes Act which was regarded by the Labour Party and the trade union movement as petty and vindictive. The Act banned sympathetic strikes, unless they were in the same industry, and replaced the process of 'contracting out' of the political levy to the Labour Party paid by trade unionists with 'contracting in' (previous legislation had forced TUC-affiliated unionists to make special arrangements not to pay a levy to Labour Party funds). Churchill agreed with the legislation, saying that the unions should 'mind their own business' and keep out of politics.

Yet Churchill's record in the immediate aftermath of the General Strike, when the NUM continued a hopeless struggle on its own, appears to be contradictory. The critical biographer Ponting points out that Churchill condemned the miners for 'indigent idleness' (this had unfortunate overtones as the word 'indigent' was written into the much-criticised 1834 Poor Law). Churchill also allegedly remarked when comment was made about the miners suffering that 'we must harden our hearts', and in the period before the NUM was forced back to work 'would countenance no sympathy for their plight'. He also, according to Ponting, wanted to repeal the 1906 Trades Union Act giving unions immunity in law if their members committed violent and destructive acts during a strike, but was overridden by his Cabinet colleagues. He becomes, in the Ponting version, the prime mover in the passing of the 1927 Act.

This hard-nosed class warrior is unrecognizable in the Gilbert version. According to Churchill's most zealous biographer,

> It was not Churchill's reputation as a strike-breaker, however, but his qualities as a conciliator that led Baldwin to ask him, eight days after the General Strike had ended, to take charge of the Government's negotiations with the miners.

Churchill is quoted as telling the NUM leaders that 'I sympathise with you in your task' when they showed some interest in the issue of productivity. He apparently backed the miners' desire for a national minimum wage in Cabinet, and certainly headed a campaign to set up national mechanisms for wage-bargaining between the coal-owners and the miners. It is on the record that Churchill was infuriated by the owners' negative attitude on this and called it 'unreasonable' and 'recalcitrant'.

CONCLUSION

As a Tory Chancellor, Churchill was something of a traditionalist. Rigorously orthodox at the Treasury, even if with reservations, he showed himself (it seemed) to be increasingly reactionary in his attitude to organised labour when it challenged his conception of the public good. Arguably it was his paternalistic streak, which seems to have grown stronger with the years, rather than his notorious opportunism which remained predominant but Churchill remains a paradox. Why, after all, would Baldwin choose him as the man to negotiate with the miners after the General Strike if he was so unrelentingly hostile to them and their cause? Perhaps he saw that the man who could bury the hatchet with Michael Collins could also do business with the NUM leaders.

timeline		
1924		Churchill appointed Chancellor by Baldwin
1925		Britain returns to the Gold Standard
1926 March		Samuel Commission reports on state of coal industry
	May	10-day General Strike in Britain
1927		Trades Disputes Act enforces 'contracting in' provision for Labour Party political levy

Points to Consider

1) **Why did Britain return to the Gold Standard in 1925?**
2) **Compare and contrast the respective roles of Churchill and Baldwin during and after the General Strike of 1926.**

7

WILDERNESS YEARS

THE 1929 GENERAL ELECTION

Churchill seems to have had some premonitions about the likely result of the 1929 general election. He himself told an audience of voters that the campaign was 'the dullest I can remember'. This was true. Baldwin had opted for a 'safety first' campaign centred on his own reliability.

Churchill, in characteristic style, tried to alarm the electorate by raising up the Bolshevik bogey once more. In a rousing, if intemperate speech, he warned the voters that the ministers of the Crown would be 'moved here and there like marionettes, in accordance with the decision of a small secret international junta', if Labour won the election. This attempt to replay the scare story of Communist backing for Labour, which had worked in 1924, failed this time. Few could seriously believe that Ramsay MacDonald, with his reverence for the British monarchy, was a closet Bolshevik.

Faced with the choice beween Baldwin, Lloyd George (who sponsored a radical anti-unemployment programme thought out by Keynes) and Ramsay MacDonald, the electorate gave no one a decisive endorsement. Labour won the most seats in the House of Commons, but the Tories had

Party	Votes	~ Seats	% vote
Conservatives	8,656,473	260	38.2
Liberals	5,308,510	59	23.4
Labour	8,389,512	288	37.1
Communists	50,614	0	0.3
Others	243,266	8	1.0
Electorate: 28,850,870		Percentage turnout: 76.1	

Table 3: 1929 election result

the largest share of the popular vote. The Liberals as in 1923 held the balance of power, and put Baldwin out of office.

INDIA

Churchill was always a great imperialist. The concept of 'King and Empire' was sacred to him. Thus it was that when successive governments in the thirties began to advocate dominion status for India (similar to the degree of autonomy within the British Empire conceded to Canada, Australia, New Zealand and South Africa), he began a fruitless and (for him) immensely damaging campaign against it. This was because his Indian campaign united him with the most reactionary elements in the Tory Party and removed him for a crucial half decade from the centre ground of British politics. 'In his India campaign of 1931 to 1935,' says Rhodes James, 'he joined hands with the type of Tory who would cheerfully have seen him hanged in 1910.' This meant that Churchill's natural allies on questions of imperial defence and international affairs remained suspicious of him.

Churchill's feud with the Tory leadership about India began in 1929 when the then British Viceroy in India, Lord Irwin (later Halifax), promised that India would achieve dominion status in the near future. This promise had the full backing of the Tory leadership, and when Baldwin supported Irwin in the subsequent House of Commons debate, a colleague noted how 'Winston was almost demented with fury'.

In fact government policy, whether Labour or Conservative (Labour was in power for a second time between 1929 and 1931) followed the pattern of gradual devolution of power to the Indian nationalists which began with the Morley-Minto reforms as far back as 1909. Churchill did not object to provincial self-government – a recommendation of the Simon Commission in 1930. But he did strenuously oppose the concession of an all-India parliament and its natural corollary, an Indian federation which the Commission also advocated. He wrote to Baldwin on 26 January 1931 resigning from the Shadow Cabinet. In doing so over the question of dominion status for India he marched, in Paul Addison's words, into 'a historical cul-de-sac'. His former colleague and ally on other issues, Leo Amery, observed how 'Churchill's belief in the White Man's Burden made it impossible for him to accept the notion that India might one day be governed by Indians'.

Was Churchill's attack on Baldwin's India policy merely a conscious attempt to seize the Tory leadership? This view of Churchill's conduct over India was certainly current at the time, and as the Indian historian Sarvepalli Gopal has noted, crude after-dinner jokes on the subject to his social confidantes did not dispel this suspicion. One was that the Indian nationalist leader Gandhi should be bound hand and foot at the gates of Delhi and trampled on by an enormous elephant ridden by the Viceroy. Gopal believes that it is

> difficult to take seriously his speeches in 1930, picturing an India in which the Labour government had handed over complete control to the dictatorship of a Congress Brahmin diarchy [the Brahmins were high-caste Hindus] which would hire an army of white janissaries with German officers to secure the armed ascendency of the Hindus.

If professional historians remain suspicious about Churchill's motives over India, it is not surprising that contemporaries, accustomed to his egotism and self-obsession, believed that his real aim was to use the issue to unseat Baldwin. The leader did indeed contemplate resignation over the controversy which may have given Churchill the support of more than a third of the Conservative Party, but he wisely concentrated his fire on the press barons Rothermere and Beaverbrook, survived a critical by-election in Westminster, and kept his position. Churchill, however, continued to attack the Government's India policy even when the economic crisis of 1931 forced the Labour Prime Minister Ramsay MacDonald (whom he impishly christened 'the boneless wonder') to form a National Government which relied on Conservative support.

From 1931 onwards, matters went from bad to worse as far as Churchill and India were concerned. The bi-partisan policy of the National Government produced a Government of India Bill by 1933 which Churchill predictably opposed tooth and nail because it conceded the concept of an all-India parliament and federation. The Bill involved more discussion than any piece of British legislation since the Irish Home Rule Acts with 4000 pages in Hansard (the Parliamentary record which contains verbatim accounts of debates). It became law in 1935.

Churchill's attempt to show that the Government 'doctored' evidence from the Manchester Chamber of Commerce to the effect that the loss of Indian cotton might harm the Lancashire cotton trade (Gilbert accepts the charge) did him little good. Neither did his son's misguided, and unsuccessful, attempt to stand against the official Conservative candidate in the 1935 Liverpool Wavertree by-election.

Party	Votes	Seats	% vote
Conservatives	11,810,158	432	53.7
Liberals	1,422,116	17	6.4
Labour	8,325,491	154	37.9
Communists	27,117	1	0.7
Others	272,595	4	1.2
Electorate: 31,379,050		Percentage Turnout: 71.2	

Table 4: 1935 election result

THE ABDICATION CRISIS

Churchill had a strong emotional attachment to the monarchy, and felt obliged to support Edward VIII's doomed effort to marry the divorcée Mrs Simpson, and keep his throne. He was howled down in the Commons, and felt that he was fatally damaged and that his 'political life was finished'. Historians have generally disagreed, and seen his foreign policy disagreement with the Tory leadership as a far more important factor in excluding Churchill from power.

timeline 1929 Conservative election defeat.
Second Labour government
1931 Formation of National Government following economic crisis.
Churchill resigns from Tory Shadow Cabinet
1934 Churchill accuses Hoare and Derby of improper conduct over passage of India Bill
1935 India Act passed. General election gives Conservative majority; Churchill excluded from office
1936 Abdiction Crisis

Points to Consider

1) **Why did Churchill march into 'a historical cul-de-sac' over India and what were the results of this decision?**
2) **After studying the material in Chapters 6 and 7, do you accept the accusation that Churchill was an opportunist rather than a statesman?**

8

CHURCHILL AND APPEASEMENT

THE LEGACY OF VERSAILLES

Britain had largely obtained what it wanted from the Treaty of Versailles at the end of the First World War. German naval power had been neutralised, German colonies fell into British hands and German reparations payments flowed into British coffers. However, it was not long before the British Government and people began to show some sympathy for the defeated Germans and increasing suspicion of their French ally, the other major European victor in 1918–19. Thus, when the French used a default on German reparations payments in 1923 as an excuse to invade the industrial Ruhr, Stanley Baldwin's Conservative government refused to support them. Conversely, in the more hopeful climate of the mid-1920s, Britain fully supported both the Treaty of Locarno (1925) whereby Germany accepted her existing frontiers with France and Belgium, and German admission into the League of Nations (1926). Successive British governments also supported the scaling down both of the amount and the timescale for German reparations in the Dawes Plan of 1924 and the Young Plan of 1929.

Churchill had not been an early critic of Versailles like Keynes or even Lloyd George. But as Chancellor of the Exchequer under Baldwin he had been responsible for cutbacks in defence spending, and was particularly associated with the notorious 'Ten Year Rule'.

THE TEN YEAR RULE

This had been laid down by the Committee of Imperial Defence in 1919, and stated that defence spending in any one year should be based on an assumption that there would be no European war in prospect for the next ten years. Churchill did insist that the rule be reviewed every year, but he also demanded, as Chancellor of the Exchequer (1924–9), that excessive defence expenditure be avoided – partly on the rather curious ground that the military hardware might be obsolete by the outbreak of war. Quite how Britain was to have an ongoing defence commitment in the meantime was not made clear (when a political colleague attempted to use a similar argument in the Commons in the 1930s, Churchill savaged him). Interestingly Baldwin, later charged by Churchill with neglecting Britain's defences, opposed the Ten Year Rule outright initially and had to be brought round by Churchill and Austen Chamberlain to the view that a European war was not imminent. Again it was Churchill in 1928 who had the Ten Year Rule placed on a continuous basis so that the Cabinet assumed 'for the purpose of framing the estimates of the fighting services, that at any given date there will be no major war for ten years'. Gilbert notes that in 1933 Churchill urged Baldwin to abandon the Ten Year Rule, but David Reynolds counters by saying that the real credit for scrapping it should go to Maurice Hankey, the Secretary of the CID, who began campaigning against the rule two years earlier. Reynolds remarks that this bizarre 'rolling' ten-year rule set the framework for British defence policy. For its later deficiencies, therefore, of which he became the severest critic, Winston Churchill must bear some responsibility.

THE NAZI MENACE

Winston Churchill will be forever associated with the struggle against Nazi Germany in the Second World War, but also with the struggle against the seemingly supine policy of the British government in the 1930s which allegedly failed to perceive the seriousness of the threat until it was too late.

When Hitler came to power in 1933, he was regarded as a rather virulent German nationalist who could be brought around to sensible behaviour by an accommodation of German grievances against the 1919 settlement (this despite an extremely prescient final despatch from the retiring British ambassador in Berlin, Horace Rumbold, to the effect that the members of the Nazi leadership were 'eccentric hooligans' and 'not normal'). Hitler's record of offence against the international community rapidly became impressive. In 1933 he pulled Germany out of the Geneva Armaments Conference (which had been vainly trying for some time to scale down Great Power armaments) and the League of Nations. In 1934 he was almost certainly behind an attempted Nazi coup in his homeland Austria, and in 1935, he defied Britain and France by introducing conscription and a peacetime army of 300,000, both clear breaches of the military clauses of the Versailles Treaty. But Hitler was also capable of seemingly conciliatory moves such as his 1934 non-aggression pact with Poland, a real surprise given Hitler's deep loathing and hatred for Slav peoples as a whole. His continuing record of aggression will form the major theme of Chapter 9.

CHURCHILL AND BRITISH FOREIGN POLICY

The word inevitably linked with the conduct of British foreign policy in the thirties is 'appeasement'. It has had a bad press, as Professor Donald Cameron Watt has recognised:

> Appeasement . . . acquired a pejorative association with the ignominious surrender of principle and the purchase of peace by the sacrifice of the interests of the weak and the defenceless.

Yet appeasement, which Watt defines as 'the defusing of conflict', is not inherently ignoble as Winston Churchill, its major opponent, pointed out:

> Those who are prone by temperament and character to seek sharp and clear cut solutions of difficult and obscure problems, who are ready to fight whenever some challenge comes from a foreign power, have not been always right. On the other hand, those whose inclination is to bow their heads to seek patiently and faithfully for peaceful compromise are not always wrong.

Few critics of Chamberlain have observed this distinction including, on occasions, Churchill himself.

Neville Chamberlain was the high priest of appeasement just as Winston Churchill was the focus of opposition to it. For Chamberlain, appeasement meant the 'double line' of trying to accommodate Hitler's grievances while building up Britain's defences (especially in the air) so that ultimately the country could negotiate from strength. Chamberlain remained convinced, despite the traumas of the period 1937–9 when he was Prime Minister, that appeasement was the only appropriate policy for dealing with the fascist dictators in Europe, and the Japanese threat in the Far East. He was dismissive of the role played by the League of Nations in international peace-keeping, suspicious of communist Russia and cynical about the prospects of any US involvement in European affairs.

Churchill's position, as historians like Alastair Parker and John Charmley have pointed out, was not initially strikingly different from that of Chamberlain or his predecessor Stanley Baldwin. In his challenging new study *Chamberlain and Appeasement*, Parker stresses that Churchill's conversion to the principle of collective security under the auspices of the League was a slow one. In 1933 Churchill was still talking about 'the interfering internationalist principles of the League' and, like Chamberlain, he was unenthusiastic about the imposition of oil sanctions by the League after Mussolini's attack on Ethiopia in 1935 (historians have highlighted Churchill's remarkably poor attendance record in the Commons when the Ethiopian issue was under discussion). Only in 1936 did Churchill really become an advocate of collective security under the League Covenant and, as Parker says, an 'eloquent ally' of those groups in Britain which opposed the Baldwin-Chamberlain appeasement policy.

CHURCHILL AND CHAMBERLAIN

Policy differences between Churchill and Chamberlain were given a harder edge by personal coolness if not outright animosity. There had been a serious difference of opinion when the two men were in government together in the 1920s over a reform of the rates system, and they were potential rivals for the Tory leadership until Churchill's eccentric line on India disqualified him.

Temperamentally they were like chalk and cheese. When Chamberlain died in 1940, Churchill was to pay him a generous tribute but privately he was known to refer to him dismissively as 'the Coroner' and 'the packhorse' of the Tory Party. Chamberlain for his part recognised Churchill's good qualities and his 'tremendous drive and imagination' but he was wary of his domineering tendencies in Cabinet, and would not have him in his own until the dire emergency of war in 1939 forced him to. He, like others, as Norman Rose wrote in his definitive biography of Churchill, distrusted Churchill's judgement and his 'mercurial' temperament. Chamberlain said that arguing with his former ministerial colleague was 'like arguing with a brass band'. Yet Chamberlain, too, is open to the accusation that he promoted nonentities who would not oppose his own highly personal view of how British foreign policy should be run.

Churchill, therefore, was excluded from office and relied on strong anti-appeasers like the former Permanent Secretary at the Foreign Office, Vansittart (sacked by Chamberlain in 1937 and given a sinecure as 'Chief Diplomatic Adviser' instead) for information and support. Chamberlain as Prime Minister was in some respects in a similar position. He distrusted the Foreign Office which he regarded as a home for 'poets and dreamers', and used personal intermediaries like the wife of his half-brother Austen to make contact with the fascist dictators, so short-circuiting official FO channels. Churchill, meanwhile, the most experienced politician in the realm and the most patriotic of men, was forced to break the Official Secrets Act by using sympathisers in the Air Ministry to obtain details about German and British rearmament in the air. Chamberlain was almost certainly aware of this but chose not to prosecute him.

There seems little doubt that Churchill's interest in, and understanding of, military affairs was badly missed in government circles in the 1930s. If it was, it was partly because Churchill was paying the price for earlier sins. Britain's defences in the meantime were left in the hands of a man who, according to a close colleague, had a mind which 'could not reconcile itself to the justification of a massive arms programme'. This judgement would not be regarded as just by many modern historians, but for the man or woman in the street it was Churchill, not Chamberlain, who epitomised robust resistance to Hitler.

CHURCHILL'S ALLIES

Churchill's die-hard position on India had distanced him from the political mainstream in both his own party and Labour, the main opposition party after the 1935 election. Alaistair Parker, however, denies that Churchill was in any kind of political 'wilderness' in the 1930s.

> He was on the contrary a highly successful, well-publicised writer and speaker. He showed as much confidence in his own abilities and insight as Chamberlain himself.

His energy was certainly astounding. He turned sixty in 1934 yet during the late 1930s, he was performing his duties as an MP, writing a multi-volumed and much admired biography of his famous ancestor Marlborough, painting regularly, building a large wall at his country house at Chartwell and making numerous trips abroad.

It was this energy, and an ability to bounce back after 1936 which put Churchill at the centre of a motley collection of anti-appeasers. And Parker is right to highlight his abilities as a journalist. He wrote regularly for the *Daily Mail*, the *Evening Standard* and the *Daily Telegraph*, the last two in particular being a platform for his criticism of government foreign and defence policy. This capacity for publicity and print journalism drew others to him. First of all, a small group of Tory MPs including his son-in-law, Duncan Sandys (who married Diana) and Brendan Bracken, a maverick Irishman who caused Winston some amusement by passing himself off as his son. Secondly, the so-called 'Focus Group' (formerly known as the Anti-Nazi Council) which included sympathetic MPs but also prominent journalists and Oxbridge academics. Estimates of the significance of 'The Focus Group' vary. Paul Addison describes it as 'a conspiracy to change the course of British foreign policy through propaganda with Churchill as the chief publicist', but Norman Rose observes that it failed to live up to expectations as an anti-government lobby group, becoming merely 'a useful channel for Churchill to expound his views'.

The Attitude of Labour

After 1936 Churchill's anti-appeasement line did attract some support in the Liberal and Labour parties, such as the independent Liberals (as apart from those known as 'National Liberals', leftovers of the former National Government who supported Chamberlain) under Archie Sinclair, whom Churchill had fought alongside in the First World War.

Hugh Dalton of the Labour Party was a trenchant anti-appeaser, and Churchill was told by a mutual friend at the end of 1936 that the Labour leader, Clement Attlee, was willing to support him 'on any rearmament programme' and that 'he admires and likes you'. But Attlee did not, at that stage, represent majority Labour opinion. The Party had convinced itself that British imperialism was as dangerous as German and Italian fascism which it purported to deplore. Consequently, although Labour wanted to stop Hitler's excesses it consistently voted against the increased military funding needed to deter him. Chamberlain and Baldwin before him were blamed for the 'cruel slaughter' in Ethiopia, Spain (where civil war broke out in 1936) and China which was attacked by Japan in 1937. Confusingly Labour attacked Chamberlain for being 'spineless' and 'immoral' while still apparently believing that colonial appeasement (restoring the German colonies taken by Versailles) would bring about a settlement with Germany.

Nevertheless Labour must be credited with the correct perception that the dictators could not be trusted, and with constantly pressing for an alliance with the USSR. Chamberlain's loathing of Soviet Communism made this a most unwelcome suggestion. Churchill found it an increasingly attractive one, and his former criticisms of the Soviet Union virtually disappeared after 1933. But there were obvious difficulties about a closer relationship between Churchill and the Labour Party on foreign policy issues. He, as indicated earlier, did not share Labour's anger about the Italian invasion of Ethiopia in 1935, or their sympathy for the Spanish Republic which came under fascist attack in 1936.

Other Allies

Churchill's allies could also be found outside the political spectrum. There were important figures in the Foreign Office like Vansittart and Ralph Wigram (who died tragically early in 1936), and also in the defence establishment. Torr Anderson, an RAF wing commander, passed on classified information on the state of Britain's airforce. Desmond Morton, whose position as Head of the Industrial Centre of the Committee of Imperial Defence involved accumulating information on German war industries, was equally helpful.

THE GOVERNMENT RESPONSE

Both Baldwin and Chamberlain recognised that they had in Churchill a dangerous critic of their appeasement policy. Baldwin, a wily operator, attempted to defuse Churchill's effectiveness by appointing him to the Air Defence Research Committee in 1935, presumably to put him in a position where he could be kept an eye on. But Baldwin did not give Churchill the job of Minister for the Coordination of Defence which was specially created in 1936 and bizarrely given to Sir Thomas Inskip (an appointment which one of Churchill's friends scathingly described as 'the worst appointment since Caligula made his horse a Consul').

Under Chamberlain, of course, Churchill had even less expectation of office which meant that with growing frustration he had to observe the crises of 1936–39 from outside the Government. He lobbied for the creation of a Ministry of Supply but when it was created in 1939, the post was given to the colourless former Transport Minister Burgin.

THE THREAT FROM THE AIR

In a famous phrase, Stanley Baldwin had said 'the bomber will always get through' and the threat of aerial bombardment hung over the 1930s much as the threat of nuclear catastrophe hung over the post-war world after 1945. Aerial warfare theorists in the inter-war period believed in the decisiveness of the 'knockout blow' which would destroy the enemy's command structures. It was also believed in the thirties that great cities like London could be devastated by mass gas attacks from the air in which hundreds of thousands of civilians would die. For a less sophisticated audience than today, the film version of H.G. Wells' *Things To Come* (with its telling sequences on urban bombing) and the newsreels at the cinema about the Spanish Civil War were a distinctly unnerving experience.

Churchill had long been interested in the problems of air warfare. He was alarmed by the pace of German air rearmament after 1933, and loud in his criticisms of the deficiencies of the Royal Air Force. The debate about the war readiness of the RAF and its strength *vis à vis* the German air force was extremely complex and confusing. The key word was 'parity' which derived from Stanley Baldwin's promise that the RAF would never be 'in a position inferior to any country within striking distance of our shores'. But what did parity actually mean? This, as Norman Rose lucidly points out, was never clear. Did such claims to equality include *all* frontline aircraft or just those actually fit for service? (On occasion the Air Staff included air frames in the figures.) No one ever seemed to be certain on this point, but when Adolf Hitler announced in 1935 that his air force had achieved parity with the RAF, many people believed him. Foremost amongst them was Winston

'Air-Minded', a cartoon by Cecil Orr (1934), published at the height of Churchill's parliamentary campaign to alert the government to the extent of German air power. He was accused of having a 'bee in his bonnet'

Churchill who announced that 'we cannot catch them up'. Ironically, Rose remarks, 'Hitler had promoted Churchill's reputation, not as a messenger of doom, but as a seer whose predictions were startlingly accurate'. This proved to be a double-edged sword. For the more that Churchill berated the government for failing to expand the RAF, the easier it was for the appeasers to retort that, if he was right, this only proved that Britain could not take Germany on in the air. Alternatively, the Air Ministry could claim, and it did, that Churchill's figures were exaggerated.

In the long run Churchill was proved right (see the table below), but in the short run, his claims seemed wildly erratic. In November 1934 Churchill told the Commons that the German airforce (the Lüftwaffe) would soon be double the strength of the RAF. In November 1935 he told his peers that Britain's true frontline strength was a mere 960 aircraft whereas Germany's was 'not less than 1500'. Three months later, Churchill's estimate of German strength (based on French figures) had shot up to an overall figure of 4000 aircraft, over 2300 of which were frontline. Other wild estimates in this period put Lüftwaffe strength at the incredible figure of 20,000 aircraft! For their part, the Nazis were adept at encouraging such delusions by exaggerating their frontline strength. On a celebrated visit to Germany the French air force chief was so alarmed by what he saw and heard that he was convinced that his force would be destroyed within a fortnight in the event of war.

Relative Air Strengths, 1939

Britain	1,400
Germany	3,000
France	800

All 'frontline' aircraft

Churchillian rhetoric on the subject abated from the autumn of 1937 onwards, as he became convinced that rearmament was 'in full swing'. Certainly Neville Chamberlain's commitment to air rearmament from the time he was Chancellor of the Exchequer between 1931 and 1937 was never in doubt, and Parker underlines the fact that the much abused appeaser had 'never denied the need to equip the United Kingdom with anything needed to ensure safe defence'. The argument between the two men was about the *margin* needed to 'ensure safe defence' and, in Chamberlain's case, there were other priorities. Unlike Churchill for whom rearmament was the only issue, Chamberlain was anxious lest Britain's precarious recovery from the economic slump of the 1930s be jeopardised by overspending on defence. For this reason, he preferred the idea of an air deterrent against the concept of sending a large expeditionary force to France and repeating the bloody slaughter of the First World War. In taking this view, Chamberlain had the full support of the Treasury.

CHURCHILL IN BLINKERS?

It is surprising on the surface that as a former Chancellor himself Churchill took such little interest in the economic and financial issues involved in starting a massive rearmament programme. More serious charges though are laid against him in Professor Watt's contribution to the definitive compilation of essays edited by Blake and Louis. In summary these are that Churchill was ignorant about the debate going on in the Air Staff about the need for a bomber-based deterrent or a fighter-based aerial defence which would also deter a German 'knockout blow'. He was, according to Watt, well informed about Britain's anti-aircraft defence weakness (there were only 12 anti-aircraft guns to defend the whole of London in 1938), yet ignorant of the fact that neither the RAF nor the Lüftwaffe were capable of launching major bomber offensives from their own bases at home. It seems pertinent to point out, however, that government and defence circles in Britain also seemed to share this ignorance before 1939. So did the Germans whose under-armed bomber formations were supposed to terrorise the British into surrender in 1940–41.

A more telling point made by Watt is that Churchill, surprisingly for a man with such close ties with both the army and navy, was guilty of concentrating his campaign 'exclusively' on air rearmament. He did not understand the revolutionary potential of the tank in land warfare (Churchill admitted as much in 1940) and, more surprisingly, the need to replace obsolescent Royal Navy battleships like *HMS Hood* when he had been so much involved with the modernisation of the senior service before 1914. Watt argues that because Churchill was not in touch with the need for such changes – especially the likely impact of air power in the naval theatre – he also had a shaky grasp of military and naval realities in the Far East. 'For Winston,' Watt remarks bluntly, 'the Pacific was a faraway country of which he knew nothing.' Another critic, Robert O'Neill, also highlights Churchill's 'determined slashing of naval expenditure in the 1920s' as one of the major reasons for the catastrophic loss of the massive Singapore naval base to the Japanese early in the Second World War. Characteristically perhaps, this contradicted a view expressed in 1921 that Japan was 'the danger to be guarded against'. Perhaps it was a case of Churchill's rigorous financial orthodoxy, a theme of Chapter 7, outweighing his strategic commonsense.

THE ROLE OF THE ARMY

Circumstances changed in the 1930s. But how was British defence policy to reflect this change? Britain had a vast, virtually undefendable empire, and by the mid-1930s three potential enemies. It seemed self-evident that she could not survive a war with a combination of Germany, Italy and Japan together. Chamberlain's answer was appeasement combined with rearmament in the air. Churchill did not demur about the latter, but Professor Watt's criticism seems to hold force about his attitude towards the army in particular.

Chamberlain's position was clear. He never forgot that his beloved first cousin had died in the First World War and was convinced that such carnage must never be allowed to re-occur. He consistently opposed the Army General Staffs' requests for a larger field army which could be sent to the continent to aid the French in the event of an attack by Germany. He believed that 'the political temper of the people of this country is strongly opposed to continental adventures'. There was to be no army on a 1914–18 scale.

Chamberlain was by no means alone in this view of the army's role. The noted military theorist of the day, Basil Liddell Hart, wrote in 1939 that the defence of France and Belgium could be left entirely to the French with no British assistance. Staff talks with the French, which might drag Britain willy-nilly into conflict as in 1914, were also to be strenuously avoided in Chamberlain's view. And a large peacetime army might prejudice economic recovery.

What of Churchill? It is hard to find definitive statements by Churchill on this issue, even though his advocacy of collective security in the 1930s would have presupposed a larger British commitment to continental defence. Surprisingly perhaps, Churchill refused to sign an appeal for national service to be introduced in 1939 on the grounds that the Chamberlain government was already working on a scheme at a time of acute international tension in Europe (see p.87). However, this scheme, as P.M.H. Bell points out in *The Origins of the Second World War*, was very limited in its application when it became law in May 1939. Full-time military service would be for six months only, almost a half (80,000) of the 200,000 conscripts were to be attached to anti-aircraft units, and none of these new conscripts would have to serve abroad unless war broke out. The delay of the call-up of these conscripts until August 1939, just before war broke out, meant that the miltary effect of the measure was minimal.

THE GRAND ALLIANCE

This chapter has traced Churchill's evolution from the isolationist of the 1920s and the 'sceptic' about the League in the early 1930s, to being the promoter of collective security and large-scale rearmament by 1936 (even if due note is taken of Watt's view that this support was too narrowly focused).

By 1938 Churchill, increasingly alarmed by Hitler's aggrandisement and his seizure of Austria in March of that year (see p.76), had moved on to advocacy of a so-called 'Grand Alliance'. This meant support for an Anglo-French and Soviet alliance, underpinned by those articles in the League of Nations Covenant which condemned aggression by any power and enjoined all states to unite against the aggressor. Smaller states like Czechoslovakia and Poland might also be encouraged to join in.

The 'Grand Alliance' would have placed the military burden on the French and Soviet armies (one of Churchill's more celebrated remarks in the 1930s was 'Thank God for the French Army'). This plan had obvious drawbacks as the appeasers were quick to point out. The Poles were famously anti-Bolshevik and suspicious of any move which might bring the Russians on to their territory. This would make it impossible to aid Czechoslovakia effectively which, with its three million-strong

German minority might be an early victim of Hitler's avowed aim to create a 'Greater Germany'.

Chamberlain and most of the Conservative Party were profoundly suspicious of Soviet Russia (as was the political right in France), and believed evidence that the Red Army had been badly weakened by Stalin's purge of allegedly unreliable officers in 1937–8. At first, Chamberlain confessed he was 'much attracted' by the idea of the Grand Alliance but once he had taken military advice on the matter, it proved to be impractical.

> You only have to look at the map [Chamberlain wrote to his sister Ida] to see that nothing we could do could possibly save Czechoslovakia from being overrun by the Germans if they wanted to do it.

Russia could not be relied upon in Chamberlain's view (nor could the USA) and neither did he trust her. France with its sharp political divisions was an unreliable entity when seen from the other side of the Channel. Even Churchill, an enthusiastic admirer of the French army, expressed anxiety to one of its leading generals about whether the defences north of the great fortifications of the Maginot Line (which covered only the Franco-German frontier) were adequate. His worries proved to be more than justified in 1940.

CONCLUSION

The weight of modern scholarship now points to the fact that the differences between Winston Churchill and Neville Chamberlain over foreign affairs and defence policy were not as great as debunkers of appeasement, like Lewis Namier and indeed Churchill himself in Volume One of his war memoirs *The Gathering Storm*, tried to suggest. It is important to emphasise the point that Chamberlain was not 'craven' or a 'coward' as the mythology about appeasement suggests. Neither was opposition to it solely Churchill's achievement as he tended to imply (*The Gathering Storm* makes no reference to the anti-Nazi 'Focus Group').

By 1939 Churchill was on record as saying that he was largely satisfied with government policy towards Germany (apart from the thorny issue of the Soviet alliance). The conflicting views about the RAF expansion had largely been resolved and the differences between himself and Chamberlain were largely (it could be argued) stylistic. Churchill wanted a much more aggressive tone to be taken with the Germans. Chamberlain felt that needless provocation should be avoided until Britain was more secure. Chamberlain is on record as saying that Hitler was 'half mad' and Churchill also wrote, in 1937, that:

> One may dislike Hitler's system and yet admire his patriotic achievement. If our country were defeated I hope that we should find a champion as indomitable to restore our courage and lead us back to our place among the nations.

These facts need to be remembered in the emotive debate over appeasement.

Points to Consider

1) What form did political opposition to appeasement take in Britain in the 1930s and how effective was it?
2) Explain the argument for the 'Grand Alliance' and the objections to it.
3) Why was the debate about aerial rearmament so fierce in the 1930s?
4) Why was Churchill an advocate of defence cuts in the 1920s but a supporter of wholesale rearmament in the 1930s?
5) 'More superficial than real.' Discuss this view of the foreign and defence policy differences between Neville Chamberlain and Churchill.

9

THE GATHERING STORM

Churchill's title for the first volume of his war memoirs was an evocative one. The subsequent problem for historians has been to decide whether this 'storm' could and should have been prevented in the years before 1939.

THE 'CHURCHILLIAN CRITIQUE'

What Professor Watt has described as 'the Churchillian critique' of appeasement was propounded in *The Gathering Storm* in 1948. It had a seductive simplicity. Hitler could and should have been stopped in March 1936 when the Rhineland was re-occupied. He was not. This offered encouragement for further aggrandisement. It duly followed with the annexation of Austria and the surrender of the Sudetenland at Munich. This, said Churchill, was 'a total and unmitigated defeat' for Britain and a betrayal of her national interest because it encouraged further aggression. At the same time Churchill argued that, at least until 1938, Chamberlain had failed to re-arm adequately in the air, or to make use of the US President Roosevelt's anti-fascist sympathies.

The sequel was predictable. Hitler annexed the Czech lands and seized the Lithuanian port of Memel shortly afterwards, and the Government's inaction killed the prospect of a vital alliance with the USSR. The years between 1936 and 1939 were for Churchill 'locust years' when chance after chance of stopping the German dictator were perversely thrown away. Baldwin and Chamberlain had between them defied the canon of British foreign policy by allowing an over-mighty Germany to dominate Europe. Churchill pressed vainly for a 'Grand

Alliance' but was balked at every turn by Chamberlain's unwillingness to make continental alliances, and in particular by his, and his Foreign Minister Lord Halifax's, aversion to the Soviet Union. Learning nothing from Hitler's bad faith, Chamberlain persisted (more secretly after March 1939) in appeasing Hitler to the eleventh hour, and beyond. Professor Watt sums up the Churchillian critique thus:

> The Churchillian critique can be reduced to three propositions: that a greater rate of British rearmament would have deterred Hitler; that a more aggressive style would have deterred him at crucial moments in his advance; and that a grand coalition would have deterred him or led to his overthrow.

Churchill was able to see that a policy of appeasement might at times be appropriate, as the quotation in the last chapter (see p.60) shows. His charge against the Baldwin and Chamberlain governments in *The Gathering Storm* and at the time was that the rearmament aspect of Chamberlain's 'double line' was 'too little, too late'. However, in making this charge in 1948 he was, according to modern historians, sometimes guilty of ignoring the genuine dilemma facing the British Government, and denigrating the good faith of those directing its foreign policy.

But does the Churchillian critique, which avowed that there *was* another way of dealing with Hitler other than appeasement, stand up to critical examination? To attempt to answer this question demands a detailed appraisal of those crises referred to in the introduction to this chapter.

THE RHINELAND CRISIS

In *The Gathering Storm* Churchill had written that the Rhineland crisis of March 1936 was 'the last chance of arresting Hitler's ambitions without a serious war'. But at the time there was a consensus in the British political parties that nothing could, or should be done about Hitler's action. This mood was best summed up by Lord Lothian's remark that Hitler was, after all, only going into 'his own back garden'. The Rhineland was German territory and hardly worth starting a war over. Surprisingly even Hugh Dalton, normally a resolute anti-appeaser, tried to put the blame on the French. While noting that Hitler had broken treaties in the most flagrant way, he said that 'the French Government have thrown away opportunity after opportunity of coming to terms with him'.

The British Foreign Office had seen the re-occupation coming. In 1935 the British ambassador in Berlin had written to his superiors that he feared that 'the Zone will be re-occupied whenever a favourable excuse presents itself'. The French too had effectively written off the zone unless they had the promise of British support in reacting forcibly to Hitler's illegal move. Seductively Hitler combined illegality with an offer of 25-year non-aggression pacts with France and Belgium. The British were seduced by the prospect of an Air Pact which might curb German expansion in the air.

Norman Rose notes that Churchill's reaction to the Rhineland re-militarisation was muted. He 'made no proposal' for a British response in concert with the French (who had a vast numerical superiority over the tiny German army) and observed that the Rhineland was but 'the smallest part of the whole problem'. Churchill had reservations but when Eden as Foreign Secretary defended British policy in 1936 by saying that this was 'a quarrel which was not ours', he described it as 'a great speech' and was impressed 'by the overwhelming consensus of opinion'. This included *The Times* newspaper, known to be closely attuned to government thinking, which came out with a notorious leader entitled 'A Chance To Rebuild'.

In Rose's judgement Churchill in 1936 was unable to offer a convincing alternative. Shorn of their rhetoric, Churchill's proposals merged smoothly into the policy the government was actually pursuing. Churchill's natural allies were also cautious at the time of the Rhineland crisis. 'We have got to be cautious,' warned Vansittart (still at that stage the Permanent Secretary at the FO), 'or we may pay for it with our national existence.' Nevertheless, the Churchillian analysis still has something to be said for it.

In a seminal specialist study in the mid-1970s, J.T. Emmerson underlined the significance of the crisis. 'Looking back on the events of March 1936,' he wrote, 'it is harder to escape the conclusion that there was only one winner: Germany, or more specifically Hitler.' The Führer's popularity in Germany was greatly increased, and the re-militarisation removed the vulnerability of the vital Ruhr industries to French invasion on the 1923 model (see p.58). This allowed Hitler to launch his four-year plan which the work of Richard Overy in particular has crucially linked to the Führer's grandiose expansionist plans. It also raised doubts in Belgium and Eastern Europe about France's reliability as an ally when it would not act against the aggressor on its own frontier.

Nevertheless, the documentary evidence suggests that no really serious consideration was given to an armed response and that Hitler could in any case (according to Emmerson) have got the de-militarised status of the zone changed in a couple of years anyway. The British Government was already firmly committed to 'colonial appeasement' whereby Hitler would be offered back the former German colonies. It even tried to get the French to return their mandated territories in West Africa to Germany. This suggestion was firmly rebuked.

Churchill's later claim, therefore, that Hitler could have been stopped in 1936 is a tenuous one that is not supported by the evidence. Parker concludes that:

> It was only later, in retrospect, that March 1936 was picked out as the moment when Hitler could have been 'stopped'. At that time it never occurred to anyone, even to those whose minds were beginning to take up ideas of 'stopping Hitler'.

In essence, Churchill was right to be alarmed by Hitler's move into the Rhineland but wrong in his later assumption that something could have been done to stop it at the time. The decision not to react had long been taken because in Britain the issue was not a vital national interest. Without Britain, France would take no action either.

THE ANSCHLUSS

Churchill's soft line on Italy certainly influenced his attitude to the Spanish Civil War (which broke out in July 1936). He supported the Nationalist rebels, led by Franco, against the left-wing republicans.

Churchill and Chamberlain's sympathetic attitude to Mussolini availed either of them little. Chamberlain persisted in seeing Mussolini as a potential moderating influence on the German leader (the true nature of their relationship was underlined by the Duce's exasperated comment in 1939 that 'every time Hitler occupies a country, he sends me a message'). Churchill also saw Italy as a potential counterweight and briefly in 1934 there seemed some hope that Mussolini would play such a role. When the quasi-fascist Austrian dictator Dollfüss was murdered by Austrian Nazis, the Duce rushed troops up to the Austro-Italian frontier to warn off the Germans. Hitler at this stage was a 'pervert' whom Mussolini described on their first meeting as looking like 'a little plumber'.

The Ethiopian war of 1935–6 changed all that. Mussolini bitterly resented British criticism, and moved closer to his fascist neighbour. The Spanish Civil War accelerated the process and in that same year, the ominous so-called 'Gentleman's Agreement' allowed Germany to begin the process of undermining Austrian independence (it sanctioned the re-appearance of the Austrian Nazi Party). By 1938 Mussolini had decided that Austria was 'a German question' although *anschluss* or union between Austria and Germany remained illegal under the Treaty of Versailles.

Hitler undoubtedly planned the reabsorption of his homeland into the Reich at some stage, but his annexation of Austria was precipitated by the courageous, if perhaps fool-hardy Austrian Chancellor Schuschnigg. Bullied and humiliated by the German Führer at his headquarters, Schuschnigg went home and called a plebiscite for 13 March to confirm Austria's independent status. Mussolini advised him against this action which enraged Hitler. An Austrian Nazi stooge (already in the Schuschnigg government under the 1936 agreement) was ordered to take over in Vienna, and German troops invaded Austria.

The Anschluss, which took place over 11–12 March to prevent Schuschnigg from holding his plebiscite lest the Austrian people vote against union with Germany, also aroused muted emotions in Britain. Austria was a German-speaking country which apparently (even allowing for a blatantly rigged Nazi plebiscite after the takeover) wanted union with its large neighbour. Chamberlain believed that the Anschluss 'had to come', and did not require anything more than a protest – deplorable though Hitler's use of force had been. He still, it should be noted, believed that Germans 'were bullies by nature', an interesting comment in the light of Watt's criticism of Churchill for being guilty of 'almost racialist antipathy towards Germans'.

Churchill had made his fears known about German ambitions towards Austria in the debate in the Commons following Eden's resignation on 21 February 1938 (actually over the handling of relations with Italy rather than Germany). 'The German dictator,' he declared, after Hitler had forced the inclusion of a Nazi as Minister of the Interior, 'has laid his hand upon a small but historic country,' warning Chamberlain that 'you will have to make a stand'.

Churchill seemed vindicated by the Austrian invasion and warned in the debate that followed that Europe was faced with 'a programme of aggression, nicely calculated and timed'. It was at this point that Churchill called for 'a solemn treaty for mutual defence against aggression in what you may call a Grand Alliance'. Yet the reality was that the existence of such an alliance – to be based, Churchill believed, on Anglo-French understanding – would not have saved Austria. The French also had long given up the hope of preserving Austrian independence, as their foreign minister had made clear in 1937. It was unlikely that the USSR would have considered Austria a vital national interest, and Italy had decisively switched its position from the sympathetic one of 1934. The chance therefore of 'stopping' Hitler at the time of the Anschluss was minimal, although it is true that proper note should have been taken of Mussolini's revised stance over the issue of Austrian independence. The idea that the Duce would be in any way a moderating influence on the Führer proved to be a complete illusion.

THE ORIGINS OF THE CZECH CRISIS

It was predictable that Hitler would begin, after the annexation of Austria to the Reich, to put pressure on the Czech Government over the Sudeten German issue. Three million Germans lived in this frontier area inside Czechoslovakia. They had not been badly treated by the Prague Government since the inception of the Czechoslovak state in 1919, but had suffered in the economic depression which had ravaged the whole of Europe in the early 1930s. This experience created a basis of support for the Sudeten German Party led by Konrad Henlein, which agitated for more autonomy for the Sudetenland.

Henlein posed as a moderate who would be content with autonomy for his people within the frontiers of the Czechoslovak Republic. He impressed even Sir Robert Vansittart, one of Churchill's staunchest allies in the battle against the Chamberlain government's foreign policy, who wrote after meeting him in 1938 that Henlein was 'a wise and reasonable man'. Churchill also met Henlein in April 1938, just after the Anschluss, and he told him that all he wanted was autonomy. Churchill was sufficiently impressed by Henlein's assurances to tell an audience in Bristol a few days later that he saw no reason why the Sudeten Germans could not become 'trusted and honoured partners' in the democratic Czechoslovak republic, the only truly democratic state in the whole of Eastern Europe. Neither Churchill nor the British Government were then aware that Henlein was in collusion with Hitler in Berlin.

THE 'MAY SCARE'

Churchill's anxieties seemed to be justified by the events over the weekend of 20–21 May 1938, known to historians as the 'May Scare'. Rumours spread in central Europe that Hitler was about to launch an attack on the Czechs and the Czech government of Dr Benes authorised a partial mobilisation of its army. France said it would honour its 1935 Treaty of Mutual Defence with the Czechs, and the USSR said it would honour its alliance of the same year if France honoured its commitment too (a crucial qualification as it turned out).

The British position was a masterpiece of obfuscation or a clever piece of diplomacy, depending on the point of view. His Majesty's Government, the Germans were informed, 'could not guarantee that they would not be forced by circumstances to become involved also'. But at the same time, the French were informed by the British ambassador that they should not rely upon Britain's assistance if France did stand by the Czechs. In such a manner, notes Parker, 'the Foreign Office made sure that British policy maintained its careful balance'. The Germans were to be kept guessing about British policy, but so were the French.

The irony was that documentary evidence now available confirms the fact that Hitler was *not* about to attack the Czechs anyway. He was enraged by the accusation that Germany had been forced to back down (despite the efforts of the British Government to muzzle any suggestion in the press that Germany had been humiliated) and days later told his military staff of his decision 'to smash Czechoslovakia'. The apparently solid anti-Hitler front at the time of the May Scare was in fact an illusion. The British attitude as described above was ambivalent, and France would not act without British support. This gave Stalin a pretext for avoiding his commitment to Czechoslovakia too.

THE ROAD TO MUNICH

If 'appeasement' has become a loaded word full of negative symbolism, so has 'Munich' – arguably the highwater of the policy itself. The ill-fated meeting in September 1938 which determined Czechoslovakia's fate derived, in Churchill's view, from Chamberlain's decision to approve the cession of the Sudetenland to Germany, by bullying the Czechoslovak Government into giving up its own territory.

But Munich was only reached in stages. First of all Chamberlain, alarmed by the 'May Scare', sent Lord Runciman (an odd choice) on a fact-finding mission to the Sudetenland which served only to open him and the British Government to German propaganda claims about alleged Czech 'atrocities' against the Sudetens. Runciman achieved little, merely demonstrating Chamberlain's penchant for using non-Foreign Office intermediaries.

Meanwhile Hitler's rhetoric was getting wilder and wilder as he threatened the Benes Government with war if his demands were not met. Ostensibly he only wanted autonomy for the Sudetens, but secretly he instructed Henlein to raise the stakes and to demand eventual incorporation of the Sudetenland into the Reich.

A significant watershed in the British attitude occurred on 7 September when *The Times*, whose editor Dawson confessed that he lay awake at night worrying about offending German sensitivities, openly suggested that the Sudetenland should be ceded to Germany. This particular kite-flying exercise almost certainly had government backing. The British Government was now, according to Ponting, adopting the dangerous policy of firstly trying to persuade the Czechs to give up the Sudetenland and secondly persuading Hitler to accept this peaceful transfer without starting a war. In this scenario Hitler had a priceless advantage over his opponents. He alone wanted a war in 1938.

Churchill now had a sharp disagreement with the government and began to follow what was effectively an alternative foreign policy. He encouraged the anti-appeasing '*bellicistes*' (hawks) in the French Cabinet and may also have secretly encouraged Benes to resist Chamberlain's advice. Predictably his demand that an ultimatum be sent threatening Germany with war was rejected.

Berchtesgaden

Unknown to Churchill, Neville Chamberlain had already decided to try personal diplomacy. He would fly, at the age of 69, to Germany to meet the Führer and discuss the Sudeten question.

The meeting took place at Berchtesgaden, Hitler's mountain house in Bavaria on 15 September 1938. Churchill was unaware that the meeting was about to take place, as was Britain's ally France. But by this time Benes had conceded the principle of autonomy for the Sudetenland. Hitler now demanded that the region be ceded to Germany and Chamberlain agreed to put this demand to the British Cabinet. They, in turn, agreed to plebiscites in the German majority areas of the Sudetenland. Churchill was unaware of the pressure that Britain was placing on the Czech Government in Prague, and Gilbert tells us that he contemplated sending a telegram to Benes encouraging him to 'Fire your cannon, and all will be well'. In the end he desisted, worried lest he should be taking on government responsibilities.

Godesburg

Neville Chamberlain flew back to see Hitler a second time at Bad-Godesburg on the Rhine on 22 September. This time the Führer deigned to come to the German border to meet the ageing premier. But even Chamberlain was shaken when Hitler demanded immediate cession of the Sudetenland by 1 October and settlement of Polish claims (for Teschen) and Hungarian claims (in Ruthenia) against the Czechs simultaneously. Chamberlain angrily retorted that if that was to be the Führer's attitude there was little point in continuing the conversation. He then had second thoughts and on the second day of the Godesburg meeting agreed to Hitler's demand that there should be no plebiscites in areas of the Sudetenland which had 50 per cent or more German-speaking inhabitants. All Czech fortifications and war materials in the Sudetenland were to be transferred to Germany. This was a vitally important point because the area contained the Czech 'mini-Maginot' line which impressed military observers who saw it. Loss of the fortifications would leave Czechoslovakia, surrounded on three sides by German territory after the Anschluss, virtually defenceless.

Churchill was enraged by the details of Chamberlain's original plan, proposing a plebiscite which would be followed by transfer of the Sudetenland to Germany if the vote was affirmative. He told a supporter, 'It is the end of the British Empire.'

The Role of Lord Halifax

Churchill now found an unlikely ally in the Foreign Secretary, Halifax, in his struggle with Chamberlain over the Sudetenland issue. He had known Edward Wood, Viscount Halifax for many years, and they had served together in Baldwin's 1924–29 government. However, they had clashed over the Indian question and Churchill opposed government policy thereafter (see Chapter 6). Halifax was a highly intelligent, extremely religious peer whose propensity for communing with the Almighty gave him the nickname in the Churchill family of 'Holy Fox'.

Before Godesburg Halifax had been Chamberlain's 'alter ego', seeing no alternative to the Anschluss and colluding with the Prime Minister's attempts to get Benes to agree to a plebiscite. The news from Godesburg however, made the Foreign Secretary uneasy. After a sleepless night on 24/25 September he concluded that coercion of the Czechs would be improper and told a startled Prime Minister at the Cabinet meeting after Godesburg that 'he could not rid his mind of the fact that Herr Hitler had given us nothing and that he was dictating terms'. Halifax went on to say that peace would be uncertain as long as Nazism lasted. 'For this reason,' he said, he 'did not feel that it would be right to put pressure on Czechoslovakia to accept.' If the Czechs accepted the Godesburg plan all well and good but, Halifax told a disturbed Chamberlain, 'If they rejected it he imagined that France would join in and if the French went in we should join them.' Nothing could have been further from Chamberlain's mind than that Britain should join the French or anyone else in the defence of Czechoslovakia, but he was deeply shaken by what Halifax had to say sending him a pencilled note after the meeting about how Halifax's 'change of view had been a horrible blow to me'.

This volte-face was not quite the earth-shaking event portrayed by Andrew Robert's 1991 biography of Halifax, and neither was Chamberlain the petulant prime minister who 'admired and trusted

Hitler' as Roberts suggests. Nevertheless the conversion was significant because Halifax, as a potential alternative prime minister, carried weight with his Cabinet colleagues. The majority agreed with Halifax that it would be better if the Czechs agreed to the Godesburg terms but that they should not be coerced. According to a colleague, Halifax now regarded Hitler as 'a criminal lunatic'.

War seemed imminent. On the evening of 27 September Chamberlain made his famous, and notorious radio broadcast in which he referred to 'a quarrel in a faraway country, between people of whom we know nothing'. (Arguments about the motivation behind this remark are best left to the companion volume in this series about Chamberlain – see p.97.) But the Royal Navy was being mobilised and trenches were being dug in public parks. War with Nazi Germany appeared likely within days. Churchill rejoiced. At last it seemed to him and his supporters that Britain was standing up to Hitler.

'A TOTAL AND UNMITIGATED DEFEAT'?

Churchill did not know his man, however, for Neville Chamberlain's resolve to preserve the peace was as single-minded as Churchill's desire to preserve the honour of the British Empire. The day after his 'faraway country' broadcast on 28 September, Chamberlain made a further attempt to get Hitler to negotiate by asking for another conference. The services of Hitler's friend Benito Mussolini were also enlisted to persuade the Führer who, in deference to the Duce, agreed to meet the representatives of Britain and France at the Bavarian state capital Munich.

The story of how Chamberlain announced this news to the House of Commons is well known (see the companion volume on Chamberlain, p.98). Churchill obdurately refused to join in the mass hysteria of his fellow MPs although he did wish the Prime Minister 'God speed'.

On 29 September Chamberlain flew back to Germany and within twelve hours he, Daladier the French Prime Minister, Mussolini and Hitler had formalised the handing over of the Sudetenland to Germany. The occupation of the Sudetenland would take place on 1 October without a plebiscite.

Three days after the Munich Agreement the House of Commons' debate on it took place. In a memorable speech Churchill pronounced the death knell of the Czechoslovak state. 'All is over' he told his colleagues. 'Silent, mournful, abandoned, broken, Czechoslovakia recedes into the darkness.' Far from being a triumph for British diplomacy, Churchill said the Munich Agreement was 'a total and unmitigated defeat'. The western democracies, he warned, would come to bitterly regret the loss of the Czechoslovak fortified line, and all their influence in the countries of Eastern Europe had 'gone by the board'. There could never, Churchill went on, be 'cordial relations' between Britain and Nazi Germany which spurned 'Christian ethics, which cheers its onward course by a barbarous paganism' (was this aimed at Halifax, the virtuous High Anglican?). Crucially, Churchill expressed his disgust at the acceptance of the principle that the international bully should prevail. What had happened at Munich was that

> £1 was demanded at the pistol's point. When it was given, £2 were demanded at the pistol's point. Finally the dictator consented to take £1 17s 6d and the rest in promises of goodwill for the future.

Was Munich a 'total and unmitigated' defeat for Britain? The Churchillian critique is seemingly a powerful one. Munich destroyed the viability of a small, democratic and friendly state. It effectively removed its armed forces from the anti-fascist front in Europe. It gave no promise of Anglo-French resolve in the struggle against Hitler, and probably ruined the last remaining chance of an alliance with the USSR (in his seminal 1984 study of Soviet foreign policy, Jonathan Haslam has not been quite so dismissive of the possibility of Soviet intervention as Professor Watt, Charmley and others). As a result of French inaction, Stalin had been in the happy position of being absolved of his commitment to the Czechs under the 1935 Soviet-Czech Treaty.

As far as Hitler was concerned Munich increased, it is alleged, his contempt for 'the little worms' (that is Daladier and Chamberlain). Valuable Czech munitions fell into his hands and, far from providing extra time for Anglo-French rearmament, Munich actually gave Germany extra time to build up its armed forces. The 'breathing space' argument is jn any case not one used by Chamberlain at the time. There is no reference to it in his personal papers at Birmingham University because Chamberlain was convinced that an understanding with Germany *was* possible. He continued to believe this until March 1939 and even beyond it.

With the passage of time however, historians have come to recognise that the argument is a finely balanced one. British commitments throughout the globe in 1938 were daunting and there was no certain hope of Soviet or US assistance. The US President F.D. Roosevelt actually signalled his approval of the Munich settlement in a two-word telegram to Chamberlain. It said, 'Good man.' The British Dominions were overwhelmingly against war over the Sudetenland in 1938 and this had to be an important factor in Chamberlain's calculations. So too were the Armed Services Chiefs of Staff who warned Chamberlain shortly before Munich that:

> To attempt to take offensive action against Germany until we have had time to bring our naval, military and air-forces and also our passive defence on to a war-footing would be to place ourselves in the position of a man who attacks a tiger before he has loaded his gun.

Norman Rose believes that: 'No responsible government could afford to ignore such advice.'

As it is well known, Chamberlain was greeted as a hero on his return from Munich (see *Chamberlain: A Study in Failure*, p.100), and we know now that this adulation was misconceived. But it did represent the public mood at the time. Of Britain's popular and quality press only *Reynolds News* came out strongly against Munich, and the Prime Minister received shoals of letters of gratitude.

MUNICH AND THE HISTORIANS

Forests of paper have been consumed in the historical debate about Munich. Two examples are selected here to present the differing sympathetic and critical perspectives on the Agreement.

In this contribution to the definitive compilation of essays on the origins of the Second World War edited by Boyce and Robertson and published in 1989, Sydney Aster writes of Neville Chamberlain and the appeasement policy that:

> Peace in Europe may have been secured in the short term . . . or the long term as Chamberlain hoped, but this was pacification which was bought at the expense of a third nation. For that reason alone there can be no defence of the Munich Agreement.

This makes the point that there was an issue of morality involved at Munich which Churchill highlighted in his House of Commons speech. But Churchill was primarily concerned with the distortion in the balance of European power both before Munich and in the settlement itself. With his romantic conception of the British past, Churchill knew that Britain had never tamely acquiesced in the domination of Europe by an over-mighty power, whether it was Napoleonic France or the Kaiser's Germany.

The view of the pro-appeasement school of historians is well summed up by Norman Rose, who argues that essentially Churchill had little more to offer other than rhetoric. 'Somewhat like Neville Chamberlain, Churchill, more passionately and with far greater eloquence, hoped for the best while preparing for the worst.'

Chamberlain always argued that to threaten without the force to back up your threat was senseless. Churchill believed that a threat might deter but that in the last analysis Britain's honour demanded that a threat be made, even if, as was the case in September 1938, the Sudetenland was not essential to Britain's security. Unlike most of his political contemporaries, Winston Churchill was prepared to go to war in 1938. That much at least he shared with Adolf Hitler.

THE FALL OF CZECHOSLOVAKIA

It was not long before Churchill's predictions about the likely outcome of Munich were proved right. But he first had to survive a concerted attempt by Conservative Party Central Office to have him de-selected as MP for Epping. This failed on 4 November when his constituents gave him their blessing in a vote of confidence. In that same month the true nature of Nazi Germany was made plain for all to see in a shocking anti-Jewish outbreak in Germany known as '*Kristallnacht*' (the Night of the Crystals).

Chamberlain was not deflected, however, from his chosen course. In the Commons he accused Churchill of a lack of judgement while his Cabinet colleagues were told that:

A good deal of false emphasis has been placed on rearmament, as though one result of the Munich Agreement had been that it would be necessary for us to add to our rearmament programmes.

This did not mean that Chamberlain had abandoned rearmament. However, it did mean that he saw no reason to step up the programme, which knocks firmly on the head the legend that Munich was designed to buy time for rearmament. In the meantime he and Foreign Secretary Halifax visited Rome in January 1939 to secure the good offices of the Duce in the appeasement process. Chamberlain was also worried, unlike Churchill, about the effect of accelerated rearmament on the economy. He told the Cabinet that the financial position was 'extremely dangerous'. Hence the need to balance rearmament with renewed efforts to reach an accommodation with Germany.

Any remaining illusions that Hitler would stand by his promise at Munich not to make any more territorial claims in Europe were rudely shattered on 15 March 1939 when German forces invaded Bohemia and Moravia on the alleged pretext that 'law and order' had broken down. Slovakia assumed the status of a Nazi puppet state under a crypto-fascist Catholic priest Tiso. Days before, Sir Samuel Hoare, the Home Secretary and a leading appeaser, had tempted fate by talking of a new 'golden age' of peace in Europe.

Chamberlain responded angrily in a speech in Birmingham demanding to know whether the destruction of the Czechoslovak state was 'the end of an old adventure or the beginning of a new one'. The measures which Churchill had long demanded such as moves toward conscription were now implemented. Guarantees of assistance to Poland, Greece, Romania and Turkey rapidly followed together with accelerated rearmament. Was Churchill satisfied? According to the generally-sympathetic Gilbert, he was not. The conscription measure was, in Churchill's phrase, 'a gesture' and an inadequate one at that. He welcomed the measures while pointing out that they were too late. The more critical biography by Norman Rose points towards consensus with the government. By the summer of 1939 he observes: 'He found himself in general agreement with the goverment's rearmament programme and defence and foreign policies.' By then Hitler was attempting to bully the Poles into ceding Danzig and the Polish Corridor.

THE ROLE OF THE USSR

Churchill had long been an advocate of alliance with the USSR despite his strong reservations about the Soviet system. Government dilatoriness and ideological prejudice held off the prospect of such an alliance until after the German-Italian military pact of May 1939.

However, when a delegation was sent to the Soviet Union in the summer no cabinet minister or front rank politician was included and the Russians drew their own conclusions. Its tardy departure was due in particular to Halifax, who could never actually bring himself to meet the Soviet ambassador in person. Andrew Roberts tries to defend Halifax by saying that he wished to avoid having to refuel the delegation's aircraft in Germany. However, he was reportedly unwilling to send the delegation to the Baltic in a Royal Navy cruiser 'in case it implied to the Russians that Britain was desperate'. (Britain's ally France certainly was, for at one point in the ensuing talks the Soviet representatives were told quite falsely that the Red Army would be allowed on Polish territory.) In the event the delegation took a week to arrive. Protracted negotiations with Stalin and Foreign Minister Molotov then failed to produce any result. By contrast Ribbentrop, the German Foreign Minister, was able almost overnight to sign a non-aggression pact, usually known as the Nazi-Soviet Pact, with the USSR on 23 August. Under its terms the USSR and Germany would partition Poland. Hitler was jubilant – certain that he now had a free hand to launch an attack on Poland (whose government had courageously refused to make any concessions on Danzig and the Corridor) because the 'little worms' of Munich would not dare to fight him without the USSR.

WAR AND OFFICE

In this assumption, logical perhaps in the light of previous Anglo-French behaviour, Hitler was wrong. Chamberlain responded to the Nazi-Soviet Pact by upgrading the guarantees of March 1939 to a formal treaty of alliance with Poland (25 August). Taken aback by this response, Hitler, also shaken by Mussolini's failure to support him, postponed the offensive for a few days.

The unwelcome news about the Nazi-Soviet Pact had in fact forced Chamberlain to recall Parliament on 24 August, his previous failure to do so having infuriated Churchill. The fleet was mobilised in preparation for the inevitable although desperate efforts to avoid the conflict continued to be made by Britain and France, invoking the aid of a motley collection of intermediaries which included Pope Pius XII, the Queen of the Netherlands, Mussolini and a Swedish businessman.

All such interventions failed. On 1 September German troops invaded Poland and German aircraft bombed Polish cities. Churchill was called to 10 Downing Street by Chamberlain and offered the post of Minister without Portfolio in a small war cabinet. Mysteriously however, the appointment was not confirmed as Churchill waited impatiently at Chartwell, his country house in Kent. Chamberlain had still apparently not abandoned his hope that the peace might be preserved. Ultimately there was a revolt in the Cabinet with resignations threatened by senior figures like Simon, the Chancellor of the Exchequer, and Hoare Belisha, the Army Minister, unless the Germans were sent an ultimatum to get out of Poland. The mood of the House of Commons, as Churchill noted, was fiercely patriotic and 'there was no doubt that the temper of the House was for war'. Chamberlain's prevarications produced a fierce rebuke from Leo Amery, a former Cabinet colleague of both himself and Churchill, who shouted to the Labour Deputy Leader Greenwood, 'Speak for England!'

On 3 September Chamberlain bowed to the inevitable and an ultimatum was sent to Hitler expiring at eleven o'clock that morning, demanding an evacuation of German forces on pain of war with Britain. No response was ever received to this ultimatum and Britain duly declared war on Germany. The French declaration followed some hours later.

Immediately after the declaration of war, air raid sirens went off all over London (it was a false alarm) and Churchill and his family (who were at their flat at Morpeth Mansions) were forced into an air raid shelter. Afterwards he went to the House of Commons where he received a message that Chamberlain wanted to see him. After expressing the hope that old animosities would be forgotten in the national emergency, he offered Churchill his old job as First Lord of the Admiralty. Churchill replied by telling the Prime Minister that he was honoured to accept and that 'we shall have them'. The Admiralty immediately signalled to all Royal Navy ships 'Winston is back'. Eleven years without office, if not influence, were over.

CONCLUSION

The debate about appeasement goes on, but the historiography has taken a sharply different turn since the 1960s. This transformation is perhaps most aptly summed up by Professor Paul Kennedy's judgement that: 'Far from finding Chamberlain's policy in the late 1930s inexplicable, it now seems quite understandable to many historians.' But the Churchillian critique, so colourfully put forward in his war memoirs lives on, although Churchill himself made no pretence that *The Gathering Storm* and the following volumes were in any way objective. Churchill gave his version of events which powerfully influenced post-war historians and political leaders alike. As late as the 1980s Margaret Thatcher, for example, still found it necessary to personally apologise to the Czech President for the 'betrayal' at Munich, and 'appeasement' is still a dirty word, especially in the USA.

Churchill's legacy, according to Professor Watt, has been 'counter-factual history' which ignores the unpleasant realities which faced the Baldwin and Chamberlain governments. Yet ultimately Churchill was right and Chamberlain was wrong, as the Prime Minister recognised in the broadcast he made to the British people on 3 September. Hitler was not appeased because in the end he was not appeasable. Whether Britain was in a position to adopt an alternative policy, and this is the major issue raised by critics of the Churchillian critique, is another matter entirely.

timeline

1936	March	Hitler re-occupies the Rhineland. Inskip rather than Churchill appointed Minister for the Co-ordination of Defence
	July	Outbreak of Spanish Civil War
	November	Rome-Berlin Axis
1938	February	Resignation of Eden
	March	The Anschluss
	May	False rumours about German attack on Czechs
	September	Munich Conference
	October	Churchill describes Munich as 'a total and unmitigated defeat' in the House of Commons debate. Attempts to de-select Churchill as MP for Epping

1939 March	Hitler occupies Bohemia and Moravia. British guarantees to Poland, Greece, Turkey and Romania
April	Conscription introduced (modified version)
May	Pact of Steel between Italy and Germany
August	Nazi-Soviet Pact
	Anglo-Polish defence treaty
September	Hitler invades Poland. Anglo-French declaration of war on Germany. Churchill returns to the Admiralty

Points to Consider

1) What was the 'Churchillian critique' of appeasement and how valid was it?
2) Was the Munich settlement 'a total and unmitigated defeat' for Britain?
3) Was the outbreak of the Second World War in 1939 inevitable?

10

CHURCHILL'S FINEST HOUR

THE 'PHONEY WAR'

Britain went to war for Poland in September 1939 but did virtually nothing to assist that unfortunate and courageous nation. Neither did the French, other than to launch a feeble offensive into the Saarland, which never fully tested the German defences in the west. Within three weeks Poland was defeated, caught between the treacherous alliance set up in the Nazi-Soviet Pact.

There followed that strange period known to history as the 'phoney war' (an American description) when there was no major fighting in the west after Hitler's rapid triumph over the Poles. During this period British activity was confined to the naval and air theatres. A rare burst of activity in December found British naval forces in opposition to the German commerce raider, the *Graf Spee* off Montevideo in Uruguay. The *Graf Spee* was forced to scuttle itself and the victorious seamen paraded through the City of London under Churchill's approving eye.

On land the severe winter of 1939–40 inhibited activity and forced Hitler to cancel his planned offensive. But after a freak accident early in 1940 when a crash landing in Belgium by a German aircraft placed German invasion plans in Allied hands, Hitler radically altered them. Now there would be an additional thrust by powerful armoured forces through the heavily-wooded Ardennes where poor quality French divisions lined the River Meuse.

Churchill pressed for the mining of Norwegian territorial waters around the port of Narvik to interrupt the iron ore trade between Germany and Sweden. (He also, like other colleagues, supported a madcap plan to assist the Finns in their 'winter war' with Russia. Fortunately for the Anglo-French the Finns collapsed before any action was taken.) This was done in April but merely provoked Hitler into a rapid strike into Scandinavia. The German navy suffered heavy losses after Anglo-French intervention but German air superiority was decisive. Denmark and Norway were overrun, and Anglo-French troops evacuated from Norway. It was at this point that Winston Churchill became Prime Minister on 10 May 1940.

CHURCHILL AT THE ADMIRALTY

Before the war Stanley Baldwin had remarked, 'Winston really understands battles.' His return to an armed service ministry in 1939 therefore seemed logical, even if the putative battles were to be on sea rather than on land. Others were less enthusiastic about Churchill's return to office. In his celebrated diary 'Chips' Channon, the maverick pro-appeasement MP and admirer of Chamberlain, bemoaned the fact that Churchill lacked 'the great dignity of Neville' and that there was 'always the quite inescapable suspicion that he love(d) war which broke Neville Chamberlain's better heart'. Certainly there was a striking difference in outlook between the Prime Minister and his new First Lord of the Admiralty. Chamberlain loathed the prospect of war, Churchill found it exhilarating. Yet the two men worked together in the War Cabinet harmoniously enough, and Churchill was ostentatiously loyal to his old rival.

Surprisingly too, the two men agreed on grand strategy. Both men believed that the vulnerable German economy would crack under the strain of war, that the Allies should wait for Hitler to make the first move on land, pursue an energetic policy at sea, keep Italy neutral and press on with rearmament. Chamberlain believed that this strategy would bring Germany to its knees by the spring of 1940. Churchill thought that 'the Kaiser's Germany was a much tougher nut to crack' than Hitler. Only later as the war effort got bogged down in atrophy (a minister was alleged to have vetoed the bombing of German arms dumps in the Black Forest on the grounds that it 'was private property'!) did Churchill become uneasy. By March 1940 he was telling Lord Halifax that 'we have never done anything except follow the least line of resistance'.

Churchill agreed with his colleagues that the war at sea should be pursued with vigour. However, his suggestions that a fleet should be sent into the Baltic and Norwegian waters mined to intercept German iron ore supplies coming from Sweden via the port of Narvik ran into professional, not political opposition. It was the First Sea Lord Pound who vetoed such a scheme until the sea lanes could be cleared of German commerce raiders and the potential U-boat menace was eliminated. David Reynolds also points out that the Foreign Office (under the appeaser Halifax) also disapproved of Churchill's Scandinavian scheme because it might antagonise neutral Norway and Sweden. By the time the approaches to Narvik *were* mined in early April 1940, it was too late as days later Hitler launched his successful strike against Norway and Denmark. Churchill was blamed for the fiasco of the Allied intervention and was, according to the noted naval historian Marder, 'a main contributor' with others to the debacle. Enemies naturally saw Norway as a re-run of Gallipoli. But Churchill's professional naval colleagues had underestimated, like him, the importance of air superiority in Norway and Hitler's capacity to move swiftly and decisively.

PRIME MINISTER

The irony about the Norwegian fiasco was that Churchill, a major culprit in its failure, became Prime Minister because of it. For Chamberlain was a more obvious target for the growing feeling of unease in the Commons about the conduct of the war. He did not help his cause by incautiously pronouncing before the Norway campaign that 'Hitler has missed the bus'. Far from missing the bus, Hitler was to move at a speed which first bemused and then routed his opponents.

The Norway debate

By coincidence the very day that Hitler launched his long-expected offensive in the west, Chamberlain was replaced by Churchill as Prime Minister. This followed the Norway debate in the House of Commons when widespread dissatisfaction with the government's handling of the war finally erupted. The debate began on 7 May and Chamberlain was greeted by his parliamentary critics with cries of 'Missed the bus!' He was immediately attacked by Leo Amery, a leading Tory dissident, in a devastating speech which quoted from another made by Oliver Cromwell 300 years before. 'You have sat too long for any good you have been doing. Depart, I say, and let us have done with you. In the name of God, go!'

Churchill loyally tried to defend the government's record but on the second day of the debate, his old mentor Lloyd George, who also demanded Chamberlain's resignation, cautioned the First Lord not to 'allow himself to be converted into an air-raid shelter to keep the splinters from hitting his colleagues'. Normally the government had a massive working majority of 250 but it now sank to a mere 81, giving Chamberlain, as Gilbert observes, 'a hollow victory'. Anti-Chamberlainites began in a rather eccentric manner to sing *Rule Britannia* when the vote was announced and shout 'Go! Go! Go!' at Chamberlain, who still had a large working majority. Nevertheless the Prime Minister was severely shaken.

Churchill or Halifax?

That same evening, Chamberlain went to Buckingham Palace to see King George VI (a great personal admirer) and told him that he would be forming an all-party government with Labour and the Liberals. This was an unlikely scenario as Chamberlain had a long history of bad relations with the Labour Party (see Chamberlain, *A Study in Failure*, p.42). Surprisingly perhaps, the Labour leader Attlee preferred Churchill to Halifax as a potential leader and certainly to Chamberlain (though we have noted Attlee's approval of Churchill's anti-appeasement line in the 1930s). His biographer Kenneth Harris has written that Attlee

> knew the Labour Party remembered Churchill and Tonypandy, but he personally remembered Gallipoli. He did not feel that the Labour Party's longstanding distrust of Churchill, mainly because of his behaviour during the General Strike, was a bar to serving under him in a wartime coalition.

The attitude of the Labour Party leadership was clearly crucial if a national coalition was to be formed. Most of the Labour leaders preferred Halifax although they would have accepted Churchill at a pinch. The public was ambivalent. Opinion polls on a possible succession to Chamberlain put Churchill behind Eden. Inside the Tory Party, still of course largely with Chamberlain despite his defeat in the Norway debate, there was much animosity towards Churchill. R.A.

('Rab') Butler, who was closely associated with appeasement as a junior minister in the Foreign Office, wrote that Churchill was 'a half-breed American, whose main support was that of inefficient but talkative people of a similar type'. There were reservations about Halifax too (he was described by Attlee in a characteristically cryptic aside in the following terms: 'Queer bird Halifax. Very humorous, all hunting and Holy Communion'). Nevertheless as Leo Amery pointed out, 'If the matter had been left to a parliamentary vote, a majority vote of both Conservatives and Socialists would have favoured Lord Halifax.'

But it did not come to a parliamentary vote. Labour made it clear that it would not serve under Neville Chamberlain who told his former Parliamentary Secretary Kingsley Wood that he would stand down if Labour, as the main opposition party, would not accept him. In this sense Professor Peter Hennessy is right to point out (in his fascinating study of wartime Britain *Never Again* [1992]) that 'the Labour Party found itself in a position to determine the fate of the Government'. Was there, however, an *eminence grise* behind Chamberlain's fall in Kingsley Wood? For in Martin Gilbert's version of events, it was Wood who lunched with Churchill on 9 May, told him of Chamberlain's personal preference for Halifax, and advised him to make evident his willingness to become prime minister.

Later that day, Chamberlain invited both Churchill and Halifax to Downing Street to put the issue of his successor before them. Churchill's version of events in *The Gathering Storm* is typically melodramatic. He conceded that he was usually a garrulous person but that

> on this occasion I was silent . . . As I remained silent a very long pause ensued. It certainly seemed longer than the two minutes' silence one observes at the commemoration of Armistice Day. Then at length Halifax spoke. He said that he felt his position as a Peer out of the House of Commons would make it very difficult for him to discharge his duties as Prime Minister in a war like this . . . He spoke for some minutes in this sense and by the time he had finished it was clear that the duty would fall upon me – had in fact fallen upon me.

Doubts have been cast by historians on this version of events. Lord Blake points out that Churchill was writing at least six years after the event (*The Gathering Storm* was not actually published until 1948, allowing some time for the publication process) and that Halifax's account, written on the actual day of the interview, makes no reference to the famous 'pause'. Here it seems is another example of Churchill the colourful propagandist at work, for although Blake concedes that there may have been a pause, he writes that 'it is inconceivable that it lasted for more than two minutes'.

Much more important in the last analysis was the fact that Halifax did not want to be prime minister. This much at least is clear from Andrew Roberts' biography. The prospect of being prime minister gave Halifax 'a stomach ache' but his real reasons for declining the post as outlined by Roberts are more compelling than the traditional excuse, put forward by Churchill, that he was a peer. Halifax, like Chamberlain, was no man of war. 'He knew himself to be "a layman" in all things military . . . Churchill, on the other hand, thrived on war and was fascinated by it.' Roberts also suggests that Halifax, long used to the more urbane atmosphere of the House of Lords, might have been 'unwilling to return to the bear-pit of the Commons' and be subjected to the sort of savaging which had brought down Neville Chamberlain.

In the event, Churchill was right in his retrospective statement that the burden of the highest office had 'in fact fallen upon me'. The following day, as German troops were unleashed on Western Europe by Hitler, Chamberlain resigned, advised the King of his successor and Churchill became, at 65, Prime Minister. All his life had perhaps been a preparation for this task. 'Fate' writes Rose, 'had preserved him for this moment, as he knew it always would.' The relevant passage in *The Gathering Storm* has the smack of real authenticity:

> I was conscious of a profound sense of relief. At last I had authority to give directions over the whole scene . . . all my past life had been but a preparation for this hour and for this trial . . . and I was sure I should not fail.

'BLOOD, SWEAT AND TEARS'

The situation facing Winston Churchill on 10 May 1940 was indeed a grim one, although he did not then know how grave it was. Neither was his political base a strong one. Many Conservatives were outraged by what they saw as Chamberlain's betrayal (he had continued to hope until

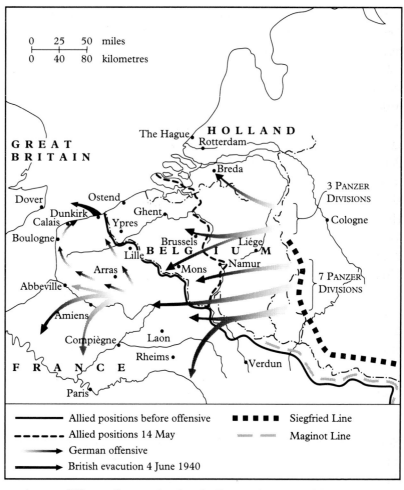

*A map of Western Europe, showing the German invasion of France, which
began on 10 May 1940 with an attack on Holland. By 21 May German tank
units had reached the coast and turned north to pursue the British
Expeditionary Forces, who retreated to Dunkirk where they were evacuated back
across the Channel.*

the last minute that he could remain in 10 Downing Street), and
pointedly failed to cheer in the traditional manner when Churchill
entered the House of Commons as Prime Minister for the first time. The
former Party Chairman spoke for many when he doubted Churchill's
essential loyalty to the late administration, which he believed was the
victim of an intrigue which 'had been going on for some time'.

Doubts were also expressed, as Sheila Lawlor points out in her study *Churchill and the Politics of War* (1994), about the quality of Churchill's ministerial appointments. Greenwood, the Labour deputy leader (Minister Without Portfolio) was known to have a drink problem and was described by one of his own colleagues as being 'very slow', while Attlee (Lord Privy Seal) was derided by a Tory backbencher for being 'poor stuff – feeble, inaudible, ineffective'. Nor were Tory appointments safe from castigation for Eden (War Office) was denounced by the Permanent Under Secretary at the War Office no less – his top civil servant as 'a poor feeble little pansy'. There was general resentment, too, about the removal of longstanding Tory stalwarts like the appeasers Hoare and Simon, and the promotion of Churchill's personal associates like Bracken and Boothby. Chamberlain, however, was retained as Lord President of the Council. He was still the Conservative Party Leader, and Churchill knew that he was little loved on the Tory backbenches and needed the fallen Premier's influence and support.

Churchill immediately sensed the need to raise the morale of the nation for the great struggle which lay ahead. Three days after assuming office on 13 May 1940, he told the British people:

> I have nothing to offer but blood, toil, tears and sweat . . . You ask what is our policy? I can say: It is to wage war, by sea, land and air with all the might and with all the strength that God can give us.

Never perhaps was a political leader so well matched, at both an intellectual and emotional level, to the crisis which confronted him. In the crisis of 1940 Norman Rose accurately observes of Churchill: 'The magnificent phrases poured out.'

DISASTER

It was as well that they did. Churchill was barely accustoming himself to the exertions and privileges of his new office when the scale of the disaster which was taking place across the Channel was made clear to him.

After 10 May German forces swept into Luxembourg, Holland and Belgium (where they swiftly captured the supposedly impregnable fortress of Eben Emael near Liége in an audacious parachute landing).

This was bad enough, but the decisive breakthrough came further south in the Ardennes where the French were unprepared for, or chose to ignore intelligence reports about the massive armoured thrust which broke through their fortifications along the River Meuse. Devastating aerial attacks on the French divisions accompanied the panzer breakthrough, while the Allied airforces were strangely inactive in the first two crucial days along the Meuse.

At 7.30 am on 15 May Churchill was awoken by a desperate telephone call from the new French Prime Minister Paul Reynaud, an old friend who had replaced Daladier in March 1940. He was astounded to learn from his ally that 'We are beaten; we have lost the battle' and replied, 'Surely it can't have happened so soon?' But Reynaud retorted, 'The front is broken near Sedan, they are pouring through in great numbers with tanks and armoured cars.' Unlike Churchill, Reynaud had a shrewd appreciation of what was going on at the Front for, as Alistair Horne points out in his definitive study *To Lose A Battle: France 1940*, Reynaud was one of a small minority in France 'who had long preached, and studied the possibilities of armoured warfare'. Churchill, effectively pleading guilty to Professor Watt's charge (see p.68), wrote of this episode later: 'I did not comprehend the violence of the revolution effected since the last war by the incursion of a mass of fast-moving heavy armour.'

After breaking out of the area around Sedan to the north of the massive fortifications of the Maginot Line, the German panzer divisions had only the flat, rolling plains of northern France, ideal tank country, between them and the Channel coastline. The British Expeditionary Force, pushed into Belgium in the early days of the campaign, was now in danger of being cut off from its home base, caught between two waves of advancing German armies.

DUNKIRK

Churchill and the Commander-in-Chief of the BEF in France and Belgium, Lord Gort, were now faced with a hideous dilemma. The BEF was under overall French command, and the French High Command wished the British forces to continue to support the French armies in their retreat from Holland and Belgium. The situation was made more grave by the Belgian surrender in late May (Holland had already fallen) which was to leave a gaping hole in the Allied line in the north. A captured German document also indicated that the Germans planned to cut the BEF off from the sea but, fortunately for it, the task of destroying the British army was ultimately left to the Lüftwaffe as Hitler lost his nerve and ordered a 'panzer halt'.

Churchill ordered 'an advance north to the ports and beaches' of the Channel coastline. The army was to be brought home if necessary and the navy was to provide 'all possible means for re-embarkation, not only at the ports but on the beaches'. The chosen port was to be Dunkirk and orders began for the evacuation of British troops from the beaches on 27 May. In the meantime Churchill tried to buoy up the flagging morale of Reynaud, actually one of the most positive politicians in the French Government, when he visited London. A touchy issue was created by the revelation on 29 May that out of 165,000 men evacuated from the beaches of Dunkirk only 15,000 were French. Churchill was in Paris, this time in another forlorn attempt to bolster up French morale, and the French Commander-in-Chief Weygand was resentful. Churchill immediately announced that equal numbers of French and British should be taken off the beaches '*bras dessus, bras dessous*' (arm-in-arm).

Churchill's eloquence could not save France now, however, even though 110,000 of the 337,000 men miraculously rescued from the Dunkirk beaches were ultimately French. The French were convinced that they had been betrayed yet again by 'perfidious Albion' and that Britain was fighting to the last Frenchman. They had a point. Of 144 Allied divisions in France and Belgium in 1940 the British contributed just ten. And the RAF had only 450 aircraft, about a third of its frontline strength, compared to the 1400 of the French air force. Churchill repeatedly, to his credit, challenged the Air Staff to send more aircraft to France. But the Commander-in-Chief of Fighter Command, Air Marshal Sir Hugh Dowding, was most unwilling to do so.

In the House of Commons on 4 June, Churchill reminded his fellow MPs that 'Wars are not won by evacuations', although he had never expected the Royal Navy and the 'little ships' (virtually everything in southern England that would float) to save more than a few thousand at Dunkirk. In his most rousing oratory Churchill told the Commons that there could be no question of a separate peace with Germany even if France were forced to give in: 'We shall fight on the beaches, we shall fight on the landing grounds, we shall fight in the fields and in the streets, we shall never surrender.' After this speech a Labour MP remarked, 'That was worth 1000 guns and the speeches of 1000 years.'

The Fall of France

Churchill subsequently grieved for 'the gallant French people' but their military plight after Dunkirk was hopeless. Outnumbered two to one, the French tried in early June to establish a front along the Somme, but the Germans broke through again in overwhelming force. Paris fell on 14 June and Reynaud resigned, replaced by the aged hero of Verdun Philippe Pétain whom the exhausted French Premier had mistakenly brought into the government to shore up morale. Pétain was a defeatist, castigating the British for letting France down and convinced that his country's plight was a result of Communist subversion. His pessimism seeped into the bones of the French Cabinet even before his appointment as leader of France.

Against this defeatist spirit, Churchill struggled in vain. He had French allies in Mandel, Monnet and the young, almost unknown general, Charles de Gaulle. The last two collaborated in the plan for a Franco-British union which would have meant that surviving French forces would be evacuated to Britain, and French warships would sail to British ports. But it was too late. It was the spirit of Pétain which prevailed in France in June 1940 rather than that of de Gaulle, and on 22 June an armistice was signed with the Germans.

The Myths of 1940

Recent historiography (the work of Young, Alexander, Doughty and others) has thrown a new light on the campaign of 1940. British propaganda around the time of Dunkirk and the Battle of France, stressed French weakness while the British remained undefeated. This was far from being the case, and Clive Ponting in particular has shown how the behaviour of some British officers and troops (admittedly under great strain) was less than heroic. Britain had its heroes in Gort and Nicholson (the defender of Calais even after Dunkirk) but so too did the French in General Prioux and the defenders of Lille. A British general made the observation after 1940 that there was not much wrong with the French army other than bad leadership and that 'nonetheless its soldiers fought'. This is an important aspect of the recent demythologisation of 1940.

Yet in another important sense it was vital *then* that the myths were believed. Britain was in a desperate position after the French armistice and high morale was essential. A feeling of outrage against the Germans took root and a pride of being 'alone' against the hated enemy Hitler and Nazism. George VI, for example, rejoiced that now Britain had no more allies to worry about and a news vendor shouted on the news of France's surrender that 'We're in the Finals now!' Winston Churchill epitomised this spirit in 1940.

Churchill posed the challenge for his fellow country men and women on 18 June:

> Hitler knows that he will have to break us in this island or lose the war ... Let us therefore brace ourselves to our duties and so bear ourselves that if the British Empire and its Commonwealth last for a thousand years, men will still say, 'This was their finest hour.'

And the people responded to Churchill's oratory. An opinion poll in June 1940 shows that 88 per cent of the population approved of him as Prime Minister. He bestrode the scene like a political colossus and enjoyed every minute of it.

MERS-EL-KEBIR

France was barely out of the war when Anglo-French relations reached their lowest point since the Entente Cordiale more than 30 years before. Churchill and his colleagues were deeply concerned about the fate of the powerful French fleet which the armistice of 1940 had allowed them to retain, but the attitude of Pétain was uncertain.

Some French naval vessels were beyond the reach of the Royal Navy but powerful units were at Mers-el-Kebir in French North Africa, within the range of its Mediterranean fleet. Churchill was determined that these ships should not fall into German hands. The local Royal Navy commander was told to give the French admiral at Mers-el-Kebir three options. He could sail his ships to a British port and hand them over, or join the Royal Navy in its struggle against the German navy. Alternatively the French could sail to the French West Indies, de-militarise the ships in port there and send the crews back to France. A fourth option was to scuttle the ships at Mers-el-Kebir.

The exact circumstances of what followed at Mers-el-Kebir remain confused, but it seems that the French wished to stand by the terms of the armistice with Germany which would prevent any of the actions demanded by the British. Churchill, therefore, reluctantly ordered the French ships, trapped in harbour, to be bombarded and sunk. In the action that followed on 3 July, 1200 French sailors died. There was much bitterness against Britain in France.

But Churchill was unrepentant. It was no time, he told the House of Commons the day after the Mers-el-Kebir action, for 'doubt or weakness'. An important message was being sent to the United States, still in an isolationist mood, about Britain's resolve to fight on, and the action against the French was, he told a representative of President Roosevelt some months later, a 'turning point in our fortunes' which made 'the world realise that we were in earnest in our intentions to carry on'.

PEACE OR WAR?

Contrary to the popular legend which surrounds the events of 1940, the British Government was not completely united in its resolve to carry on the fight with Nazi Germany.

The context of the hour needs to be recalled here. France had been defeated, the USA showed no signs of entering a European conflict, and the USSR was effectively an ally of Hitler. No one outside Britain expected it to survive a Nazi onslaught in 1940, an attitude summed up in General Weygand's expectation that 'in three weeks Great Britain will have its neck wrung like a chicken' (this elicited Churchill's famous response later in the war: 'some chicken, some neck').

Was a negotiated peace contemplated with Germany in the desperate circumstances of 1940? Churchill was more sanguine than some of his colleagues about the likelihood of US intervention in the war, but he agreed with them and the Chiefs of Staff that it was essential for the long-term survival of the British Empire. He was already corresponding with President Roosevelt under the quaint sobriquet 'formal naval person' (a reference to their working relationship in the First World War when both had responsibility for their respective navies) because he recognised the vital importance of US opinion. In the short run, however, Churchill did not reject the possibility of a negotiated peace with Germany in the summer of 1940 if the terms were right.

Alistair Parker's statement that 'German peace feelers were brushed aside with scant evidence of interest in them from anyone other than R.A. Butler and the Duke of Windsor' must now be open to question. True, Butler was rebuked at the time of the French surrender for giving a Swedish diplomat the impression that Britain would sue for terms, but documents now available indicate that Cabinet discussions between 26 May and 28 May 1940 show that Churchill was involved in discussing the possibility of keeping Mussolini out of the war by making concessions (the Italian declaration of war eventually came on 10 June when France was on its knees). Halifax took the view that it was not, in the dire situation in late May, 'a question of imposing a complete defeat upon Germany but of safeguarding the independence of our own Empire and possibly that of France'. He went on to ask Churchill whether, if he were satisfied 'that matters vital to the independence of this country were unaffected, he would be prepared to discuss terms'. Churchill's reply, by contrast with what he was vigorously saying in public, did not reject the idea of negotiation out of hand. He merely said that he would not agree to 'any negotiations that might lead to a derogation of our rights and power'.

Thereafter, as Sheila Lawlor points out in her detailed study, there was unanimity of purpose among the leading figures in the government. When, on 10 July, further German peace-feelers reached the British Government via its minister in Switzerland, Halifax advised that no reply should be sent, and his colleagues concurred. Neither did Halifax favour any response to Hitler's Reichstag speech of 19 July when he made peacelike noises. Neville Chamberlain, too, suspected by some at the time of defeatism, was disgusted by the rapidity of the French collapse but wanted to 'fight on . . . till other forces can be mobilised, perhaps the USA'. Both he and Churchill shared the illusion that the German economy might collapse even now under the strain of war.

Nevertheless, it was plainly not a true version of events which appeared in Churchill's war memoirs. Subsequently Churchill wrote 'the supreme question of whether we would fight on alone never found a place upon the War Cabinet agenda'. Churchill was clearly irritated by what he regarded as Halifax's sanction of R.A. Butler's defeatism in June.

Halifax was therefore removed from his post as Foreign Secretary in December 1940 and sent to be ambassador in Washington.

Andrew Roberts believes that Churchill saw Halifax as a potential rival, with considerable parliamentary support, who might one day oust him as he himself had ousted Neville Chamberlain. He also, Roberts alleges, wanted to replace Halifax, whom he could not bully, with Eden whom he could: 'The Rogue Elephant was finally savaging the weakened old elephant to establish himself as undisputed master of the herd'. If this was part of Churchill's master-plan he had already been assisted by Neville Chamberlain's death in November 1940. The course of events had by then made Churchill the hero of the nation, and he was able to quietly succeed his old adversary as leader of the Conservative Party.

THE BATTLE OF BRITAIN

One of the reasons why Winston Churchill was in such an unassailable position by November 1940 was that Britain had faced, and seen off, a German invasion threat in the summer and autumn of 1940.

Once Hitler's peace-feelers had been rejected, it was open to him to force Britain out of the war by invading the British Isles. After Dunkirk, the British army was in too poor a shape to prevent this, having left most of its heavy equipment and many of its best troops in France. The onus, therefore, fell on RAF Fighter Command under Sir Hugh Dowding, to prevent the Lüftwaffe securing control of the skies over southern England. The German admirals, still shaken by losses in the Norway campaign, made it clear that they would not risk an invasion in the face of Royal Navy superiority without the elimination of the RAF. 'Operation Sea Lion,' as the Germans called it, would not be launched until the Lüftwaffe had swept the skies of Hurricanes and Spitfires.

Dowding was a difficult, diffident man who lacked the extrovert martial qualities which Churchill admired in service chiefs. But he had tenaciously resisted Churchill's demand during the Battle of France that more fighter squadrons should be sent across the Channel (even producing a somewhat dubious chart to demonstrate the rate loss of British squadrons in France). Now was the hour of supreme crisis for Dowding and his mostly very young fighter pilots in the short span between July and mid-September 1940. Historians have speculated about whether 'Sea Lion' was a bluff by Hitler, and pointed out that the Lüftwaffe fighters could spend minimal time over southern England. But in the end, the German failure to destroy the RAF was a victory for superior technology, and tremendous daring and courage. When asked by Göring what he needed to win the air battle in 1940, the Lüftwaffe ace Adolf Galland greatly irritated the portly Reich Marshal by replying 'Give me a squadron of Spitfires.'

Churchill, as always, was hyperactive in a crisis, dreaming up schemes to set fire to the sea, and thrilling his radio audience on the BBC with thundering rhetoric. But he fully recognised the debt Britain owed in 1940 to Dowding's young pilots. 'Never,' he said, 'in the field of human conflict has so much been owed by so many to so few.' The myth of 'the few' in 1940 lives on, and it deserves to do so. On 17 September 1940, after his air force had failed to break the resolve of the RAF and suffered unacceptable losses, Hitler postponed 'Operation Sea Lion' indefinitely. Instead he attempted to terrorise the British people by persistent bombing, 'the Blitz' on London being its sharpest manifestation. This was a task for which the Lüftwaffe was not properly equipped but London, Coventry, Birmingham and many other British cities still suffered severely. The popular slogan, encouraged by Churchill in his visits around bombed-out areas, was that London 'can take it'. The reality was that in the East End in particular, morale sometimes came close to cracking. But somehow Churchill did still epitomise Britain's resolve in the year between the French surrender and Hitler's attack on the USSR when the country truly was 'alone'.

timeline	1939	September	War between Britain and Germany
		December	*Graf Spee* scuttles itself in Montevideo
	1940	April	Hitler attacks Norway and Denmark following British mining of Norwegian waters
		May	Fall of Chamberlain government, Churchill Prime Minister. Hitler invades France and the Low Countries
		May-June	Dunkirk evacuation. Churchill reminds House of Commons that 'wars are not won by evacuations'

June	France signs armistice with Germany. Mers-el-Kebir action. Part of French fleet sunk
July	Battle of Britain begins
September	Hitler calls off 'Operation Sea Lion'
November	Death of Neville Chamberlain
December	Halifax sacked as Foreign Secretary

Points to Consider

1) Examine Churchill's personal role in the Norway campaign of 1940 and account for its failure.
2) How and why did Winston Churchill become Prime Minister of Britain in May 1940?
3) 'Arm-in-arm' (Churchill). Why did the Anglo-French relationship in 1940 prove to be so unfraternal in the end?
4) What problems did Churchill face in asserting his political leadership in 1940 and how successful was he?
5) Was there an attempt to extend the appeasement of Germany in Britain in 1940?

11

WARLORD

The term 'warlord' seems to have more appropriate application to leaders of totalitarian societies like Germany and the Soviet Union. But even though wartime Britain was a democracy, it does convey quite accurately the sense in which Winston Churchill dominated the scene. There was opposition to his leadership during the war both in Parliament and the press but it was muted in the face of Churchill's overwhelming authority. He was not overly interested in domestic policy, but in the military sphere generals were sacked because Churchill did not like them and strategic decisions were affected by the Prime Minister's obsessions and prejudices. Ultimately Churchill's power was only circumscribed by the fact that Britain acquired allies who were far more militarily powerful than she was.

THE WAR LEADER AT WORK

Churchill's leadership methods make a fascinating study. He was never an easy man to work for as this revealing passage from John Colville's *Downing Street Diaries* shows (Colville was Churchill's Private Secretary during the war).

> In the war years, when feeding was difficult, he thought nothing of keeping the Cabinet in their seats until, for them, all hope of getting any food had passed. Equally, it never occurred to him to suppose that anybody might be tired or over-worked. He thought nothing of sending for one in the temporary sanctuary of one's bath about some trivial point which could well have waited until one was dressed.

The point though that Colville makes is that Churchill's staff would accept treatment from him which they would not tolerate from anyone else. Often impetuous and woundingly curt with his staff, Churchill was generally careful to make amends in some way, although he could never actually bring himself to apologise.

Sometimes, when his manic energy caused him to expect too much of others, the mollifying influence of Clementine had to be brought to bear. Not long after he became Prime Minister in 1940 his wife wrote to him:

> I must confess that I have noticed a deterioration in your manner; and you are not so kind as you used to be. It is for you to give the orders and if they are bungled . . . you can sack anyone and everyone.
> Therefore with this terrific power you must combine urbanity, kindness and if possible Olympic calm . . . you won't get the best results by irascibility and rudeness.

'No doubt,' Norman Rose observes, 'this affectionate appeal had an immediate, sobering effect but it did not stem the flow of complaints.' To expect 'Olympic calm' from Churchill was to expect too much, although Colville notes that while often impetuous, Churchill generally pondered long over his decisions.

His day-to-day working methods bordered on the bizarre. Important callers would often be received in bed as R.A. Butler (a reprieved, if not totally forgiven appeaser) tells us in his memoirs *The Art of the Possible*. Butler was summoned to Downing Street on several occasions to see Churchill in this mode. But from being a sharp critic of Churchill, Butler became a reluctant admirer. His technique, he observed in his memoirs, was

> to violently attack a Department from which he wants to get good results . . . Those who say his only strong suit is in making speeches are wrong. I do not think he is by nature an administrator, but he certainly forces the issue on the administrators.

Butler was a perceptive critic for Churchill was not a natural administrator and his tendency to ramble in Cabinet or committee meeting could be infuriating. Colleagues noted how Attlee, the Deputy Prime Minister, conducted Cabinet business far more efficiently (even if

Churchill once curtly dismissed him as 'a modest little man, with plenty to be modest about').

The Prime Minister's work habits were, therefore, *sui generis*. So were his eating habits. He was always overweight because he ate and drank too much (especially champagne but also liberal supplies of watered down whisky which he would sip throughout the day – Nazi propaganda claims about his alleged alcoholism were, however, just propaganda). But despite his dietary excesses, Churchill was reinvigorated, like many leaders, by power, and he was a man who liked both the exercise and trappings of power. These could include an air marshal's uniform but also his favourite 'siren' suit, a sort of all-purpose zip-up romper suit, which Churchill wore on many occasions. On other days Churchill would embarrass visitors by greeting them in a vest, and on one celebrated occasion President Roosevelt was confronted with a totally nude Prime Minister!

Most people found these eccentricities endearing but they never detracted from Churchill's grasp on power, which was all embracing. Some like Maurice Hankey, who had worked closely with Lloyd George in the First World War, found Churchill's domination of wartime decision-making unhealthy. It is a moot point whether this state of affairs was more a result of Churchill's undoubted egomania, or of his total dedication to the war effort which prompted much-tried staff to condone his outbursts of rudeness.

Whatever his leadership flaws, however, there is no doubt that Churchill retained the esteem of the vast majority of the British public in the crisis years from 1940 to 1942. He gave them, John Charmley (not an uncritical source) tells us, 'something at once human and superhuman; a symbol to a people battered almost beyond endurance that all would come right'. For the crowds in Britain's bombed-out cities, who might, in the past, have seen him as a knee-jerk reactionary, he had become 'Good ole Winnie'. Churchill retained this affection even though his own prediction that he had nothing to offer in those early years but 'blood, sweat and tears' came resoundingly true.

A YEAR OF PERIL

The year between the French armistice in June 1940 and Hitler's attack on the Soviet Union in June 1941 was the most perilous period of the war for Churchill and the British people. In the winter of 1940–1 the Lüftwaffe was pounding British cities (over 300,000 civilians died in air raids in the Second World War), and German U-boats were sinking appallingly large numbers of British merchant ships in the so-called 'Battle of the Atlantic'. Churchill admitted in his memoirs that it was the U-boat menace that most alarmed him in the war.

Churchill was desperate therefore, as he had been during the 'phoney war', to strike back at the Axis powers in some way, and Mussolini's greed and exaggerated belief in Italian military prowess came to his aid. In November 1940 the Italian dictator tried to take advantage of Britain's predicament by striking at British Egypt from Libya (then an Italian colony), but inept tactics allowed a much inferior force under General O'Connor to rout his army. It was speedily driven back to its starting point and beyond by O'Connor's fast-moving motorised forces.

Here was an opportunity perhaps to drive the Axis forces out of Africa altogether before any substantial German forces could be sent to assist their badly-led, badly-armed allies. Or so it seemed. But Churchill had other priorities as Mussolini had also conspicuously failed to conquer Greece when he attacked that country in October 1940.

CHURCHILL AND THE BALKANS

British policy-makers faced a dilemma. British assistance to Greece might provoke German intervention (which was what the Greeks feared so that initially they rejected Churchill's offer of aid), and prejudice victory in the African desert. Alternatively, failure to assist the Greeks might drive Turkey, Yugoslavia and other East European states decisively into the Axis camp.

Churchill ultimately took the decision to send help to Greece and hold back a further British offensive in North Africa. In March 1941 the Germans predictably intervened. The British army was unable to stem their advance and Greece was rapidly overrun by the Wehrmacht. Churchill's hopes of continuing the struggle on the island of Crete proved to be illusory, as it too was taken by the Germans, uniquely by airborne assault although many German paratroopers died.

Did Churchill raise false hopes in Greece? And was he equally at fault in encouraging the pro-British anti-German coup in Yugoslavia which overthrew the Regent Paul who was cautious rather than pro-German, and replaced him with the young King Peter who sympathised strongly with Britain? A traditional analysis might see Churchill's alleged encouragement of these 'sideshows' as a repetition of the Gallipoli syndrome – that is, costly and unsuccessful adventures away from the major theatres of war. (Yugoslavia was quickly invaded by Hitler after the palace coup, and Belgrade pitilessly bombed.) Documentary evidence challenges this view.

Churchill did have a propensity for dreaming up schemes to invade Axis territory away from France and Belgium. This was for two reasons. Firstly, Britain was in no position to invade the mainland of Europe in 1940-41. Secondly, he was obsessed with the fear that an invasion of France would result in a repetition of the carnage of trench warfare he had personally experienced in the First World War.

However, it is now clear that Churchill was not the manic enthusiast for Mediterranean and Balkan sideshows as is sometimes portrayed. Churchill did support intervention in Greece when the Italians invaded in 1940 but some historians have argued that by March 1941 he had become more cautious. Eden (the Secretary of State for War), by contrast, is alleged to have become the greater enthusiast for intervention after initial reluctance to divert forces from North Africa. And the Chiefs of Staff, also reluctant at first to divert forces, accepted the politicians' view that some assistance to Greece was needed, if only to encourage other Balkan states like Turkey and Yugoslavia to stand up to Germany.

BRITAIN AND THE USSR

On one decision Churchill had no impact. On 22 June 1941 German forces invaded the Soviet Union and Britain at last had a powerful ally. Churchill had never made a secret of his opposition to the oppressive Communist system in Russia but he told the House of Commons that 'If Hitler had invaded Hell I should at least give the Devil a favourable reference in the House of Commons'. It followed that Britain would afford the USSR all available assistance. Churchill's first reaction, however, might have been to doubt whether the Soviet Union was going to survive at all, as Hitler's armies drove across that vast country with frightening speed. By November 1941 the German panzers were at the gates of Moscow, Leningrad was under siege and whole Soviet armies had either been destroyed by the Wehrmacht or taken prisoner.

Churchill had long been an opponent of the Soviet system, but he had also, in the 1930s, been a strong supporter of a Soviet alliance. He immediately acknowledged the tensions in the relationship caused by old ideological enmity, by saying after Hitler invaded Russia that 'This is no class war, but a war in which the whole British Empire and Commonwealth of Nations, is engaged without distinction of race, creed or party.' As Martin Kitchen points out in a perceptive article written in 1987, Churchill put too much faith in the value of a good personal relationship with the Soviet dictator Stalin. 'I like that man' he once remarked after a personal interview, but it is clear that by the end of the war the Prime Minister had grave anxieties about Stalin's long-term objectives.

Nevertheless his policy towards the USSR during the Second World War is open to serious criticism. There was no contingency plan in 1941 to allow for a Soviet defeat (which many in the British military expected) and Churchill consistently underestimated the Soviet desire to retain the conquered Baltic states and eastern Poland as, at the very least, client states. Neither did he ever realise the importance of the 'Second Front' for the USSR which would draw off German troops from the Eastern front. Stalin constantly complained about the alleged capacity of the British, and later the Americans to fight to the last Red Army soldier. It was also true, as Kitchen points out, that actual British aid to the embattled Russians was relatively small, even if sent at the cost of gallant British merchant seamen's lives. This gave the British little leverage in Moscow, and Stalin's suspicions were aroused by what he regarded as Churchill's frivolous concern with the war in the Mediterranean theatre.

In Churchill's defence it must be acknowledged that he tried hard to bury his old suspicions of the USSR in the overriding interest of winning the war against Nazi Germany. There is no reason to doubt that Churchill ever wavered from this imperative, and Kitchen concludes that he was 'neither a wanton antagonist of the Soviet Union, nor did he mindlessly appease them'. Stalin was in truth never an easy ally, harbouring as he did deep suspicions about British motives. In a revealing aside later in the war Stalin told a Polish leader, 'Churchill did not trust us and in consequence we could not fully trust him either.'

Churchill would doubtless have responded by saying that it was Soviet behaviour which created this mistrust.

As it was, Britain and the USSR became allies out of need in moments of dire national emergency. Perhaps Churchill put his finger on the nature of relations with Russia when he said in a 1930 radio broadcast: 'I cannot forecast to you the action of Russia. It is a riddle wrapped in a mystery inside an enigma; but perhaps there is a key. That key is Russian national interest.' Conversely, and this equally is central to any study of Churchill's attitude to the USSR, he would, as Robin Edmonds puts it, have 'gladly strangled Bolshevism at birth'.

THE US ENTRY INTO THE WAR

Aggressive Japanese behaviour in the Far East had been a characteristic of the 1930s. In 1931 the Japanese had attacked and annexed Manchuria, and in 1937 they had launched a new offensive which culminated in the capture of China's main cities. A further offensive along the Soviet-Japanese frontier in 1938–9 failed and the Japanese began an internal debate about whether their territorial aggrandisement should focus on China or the inviting targets presented by the British, Dutch and French colonies in the Far East. Broadly speaking the army chiefs favoured a 'strike north' policy against China and the USSR, and the navy advocated a 'strike south' policy against the European colonies and the other significant Pacific Rim power, the United States of America.

Relations between the USA and Japan worsened in 1940–1, as the Japanese compounded their aggression against China by a virtual annexation of French Indo-China by now ruled by the Vichy collaborationists. A trade embargo imposed by the Americans did not rein in Japanese expansionism, and arguably it sharpened the aggressive mood of their military which was not influenced by the seemingly ambivalent attitude of the god Emperor Hirohito (whose central role in these events remains a matter of controversy).

Churchill, as has been seen, was unduly complacent about the Japanese threat earlier in his career. He did not demur from the Chamberlain government's attempt to appease Japan in the 1930s, but retained illusions about the security of the British position in the Far

East. He also, of course, hoped against hope that the USA could be brought into the war against Hitler despite a profoundly isolationist feeling in the USA during most of the period up to 1941.

This wish was fulfilled on 7 December 1941 when the major US naval base at Pearl Harbor in Hawaii was attacked by the Imperial Japanese airforce which sank several warships and effectively immobilised the Pacific fleet (although fortunately the aircraft carriers were at sea). The USA declared war on Japan the next day. There has been a good deal of controversy about whether President Roosevelt had prior knowledge of the planned Japanese attack, but chose not to act so as to take the American people united into the struggle against Japanese imperialism. More pertinently there are doubts about Churchill's own position. Did he deliberately fail to pass on information from British Intelligence pointing to the likelihood of a Japanese attack to ensure that the USA would be drawn into the war? This question cannot be answered at present, as the relevant intelligence files remain closed to historians.

Days after Pearl Harbor Hitler declared war on the United States. While the declaration can be attributed to Hitler's misinformed and grotesque assumptions about American effectiveness and decadence, it was hardly the gargantuan blunder put forward in traditional explanations.

The reality was that for some considerable time US neutrality had been very partial indeed. In February 1941 Roosevelt's imaginative gesture whereby 'lend-lease' arrangements were made between Britain and the USA was formalised. Roosevelt had already promised at the end of 1940 that the USA 'must be the great arsenal of democracy' and he now fulfilled his promise. America would supply Britain's military needs (put at 24 million tons of war supplies) and postpone payment until after the war. It should be noted that the US position was not altogether altruistic, for Britain had to pay for everything it could in gold and by the sale of its assets in the United States. It was, as Martin Gilbert says, 'a hard bargain'. But Churchill was grateful nonetheless. In a message to the American President on the day the Lend-Lease Bill passed through the House of Representatives in Washington he said: 'Neither the sudden shock of battle, nor the long-drawn trials of vigilance and exertion will wear us down. Give us the tools, and we will finish the job.'

In August 1941 Churchill and Roosevelt had met in Newfoundland and in addition to US promises to send extra aid to the British and the

Russians, a new commitment was made to provide destroyer escorts for convoys carrying supplies between the USA and Britain. Privately Roosevelt told Churchill that American warships had orders to sink German U-boats if they came within 200 miles of a convoy. US pilots were also flying bombers across the Atlantic to Britain.

CHURCHILL AND ROOSEVELT

After his meeting with Roosevelt in Newfoundland, Churchill remarked that he had 'established warm and deep personal relations with our great friend'. The American historian Warren F. Kimball points out that it was in fact Roosevelt who had previously initiated their personal correspondence because he wanted to be on personal terms with a likely successor to Neville Chamberlain as prime minister. Kimball also casts some doubt on the actual closeness of the relationship. Roosevelt regarded Churchill as in many respects a hopeless reactionary leftover

Churchill and Roosevelt's first wartime meeting, Newfoundland, August 1941

from the Victorian era, although he was glad that such 'a wonderful old Tory' was 'on our side'. Even Churchill ruefully admitted that 'in the White House I'm taken for a Victorian Tory'.

Before US entry into the war Churchill was worried that domestic considerations (Roosevelt had to appease isolationist feeling to get re-elected in November 1940) might so delay American involvement that Russia would be defeated by Hitler. This, he told Roosevelt's representative in Britain, Harry Hopkins, could mean that 'civilisation and culture might be wiped out'.

In retrospect it is unsurprising that there were tensions between the two new allies. Roosevelt was a genuine anti-imperialist who believed that the British Empire had had its day and should be broken up. Churchill had always been a vehement supporter and defender of that empire who had not come into office, he said, 'to preside over the liquidation of the British Empire'. Fortunately for the health of the alliance the anti-fascist credentials of the two men were strong enough to paper over any ideological cracks in the search for victory over Hitler and the Japanese.

ANGLO-AMERICAN STRATEGY

The immediate dilemma facing the Anglo-American partnership in the winter of 1941–2 was two-fold: how to most effectively aid the USSR in its life and death struggle with the Wehrmacht on the Eastern Front, and how to deal with the Japanese threat in the Far East unleashed after Pearl Harbor.

While it was ultimately agreed that there should be a 'Europe first' strategy with the Far East taking second place in the scheme of things, there were clear differences in perspective between the British and American positions. Leading figures in the US armed forces like General George C. Marshall and General Eisenhower, did not share Churchill's strategic priorities. These differences have been admirably summed up by the American historian Stephen Ambrose in the Blake-Louis compilation:

> Churchill's idea was to hit the Germans where they were not, on the periphery of their conquered empire, in Norway, North Africa, the Balkans. Eisenhower's idea (and of course here he was in full support of his US Chief of Staff George C. Marshall) was to hit the

Germans where they were, in northern France, then on to the Rhine and the Ruhr.

President Roosevelt and the American military hoped for a limited cross-channel landing in France, probably on the Cherbourg peninsula in 1942. But this suggestion was vetoed by Churchill and the British Chiefs of Staff on the grounds that the effort would be too small to materially assist Stalin who was facing new German offensives in the summer of 1942. In reality Churchill feared a landing in France because, as he told Eisenhower later, he had dreams in which 'the tides flow red with blood of American and British youths' (they had indeed flowed red with Commonwealth blood at Gallipoli).

NORTH AFRICA

Instead Churchill pressed the claims of the North African theatre where the British had been hard pressed in 1941–2 by General Erwin Rommel, arguably Germany's best general of the war, and his Afrika Korps. The fall of the great British base at Tobruk to Rommel in June 1942 with its large garrison (opening Egypt to possible invasion and with it, the loss of the vital Suez Canal) allowed Churchill to win Roosevelt around to 'Operation Torch'. This plan provided for an Anglo-American landing in French North Africa which would complement a simultaneous drive by the British 8th Army from Egypt. Churchill had been dissatisfied with the performance of Generals Wavell and Auchinleck in this middle eastern theatre. They were alleged to be lacking in fighting spirit. Instead Alexander was appointed Commander-in-Chief in the Middle East, and the abrasive Bernard Montgomery as Commander of the 8th Army. This abrasiveness impressed Churchill, who had taken an unreasonable dislike to the more reflective Wavell. 'If he is disagreeable to those about him, he is also disagreeable to the enemy' Churchill remarked. In fact Montgomery was an exceedingly cautious general, even with overwhelming material and numerical superiority, as the Germans well knew.

In October 1942 Montgomery launched a counter offensive at El Alamein against the Africa Korps, soon deprived of its outstanding general and weak in tanks and air support. Early in November 'Operation Torch' was put into effect in the teeth of American military objections (Eisenhower in an uncharacteristically melodramatic comment called the day of its approval 'the blackest day in history'). 'Torch' succeeded but at great cost, as the Americans had warned, in terms of wasted time and resources. General Marshall began to refer disparagingly to the 'suction pump' of the Mediterranean theatre which diverted resources away from the western European and Pacific theatres. But Churchill pointed to the Dieppe raid, designed to test out German coastal defences in France, which was a catastrophic failure costing many Canadian lives.

THE 'FREE FRENCH'

Churchill had been encouraging General de Gaulle's 'Free French' (founded in 1940), and also set up the Special Operations Executive to assist resistance in France and Occupied Europe with the admonition 'Set Europe Ablaze!'. De Gaulle proved, with his prickly awareness of French 'honour', to be an awkward ally, but Churchill (unlike Roosevelt who loathed him) could appreciate his good patriotic qualities. In the end the General was to be accepted as leader of all French resistance forces.

THE CASABLANCA CONFERENCE

The decision to give priority to a 'Mediterranean Strategy' was formalised at the Casablanca Conference in Morocco in January 1943. Stalin was unable to attend because of the crucial struggle on the Eastern Front at Stalingrad, but Churchill and Roosevelt decided that victory in North Africa, which would be complete in 1943, must be followed up by an invasion of Sicily and, if that went well, mainland Italy too. Churchill was in partial agreement with the British Chiefs of Staff who believed that 'the Mediterranean gives us far better facilities for wearing down German forces both land and air, and of withdrawing [German] strength from Russia'. Roosevelt by contrast went against his military advisers who backed 'Operation Roundup' – an invasion of France in 1943. But the British military were convinced that the lack of troops and landing-craft available for 'Roundup' would make it impossible to attempt such a landing. Churchill, characteristically perhaps, would have liked to have launched some sort of an invasion of France even if only as a subsidiary to an invasion of Italy. He thought the Chiefs' assessment too pessimistic but went along with it. Clearly something had to be done to placate Stalin, then faced with a struggle against some three million Axis troops in Russia. The North African theátre paled into insignificance in comparison.

The other important decision which emerged from the Casablanca Conference (belatedly and begrudgingly attended by de Gaulle) was that the Allies demanded the 'unconditional surrender' of Germany, Italy and Japan. Whether this demand stiffened German resistance and discouraged the divided anti-Nazi opposition inside Germany is a moot point. Much ink has been spilt by historians on the wisdom of the decisions made in Morocco. Charmley in particular has speculated about whether the launching of 'Roundup' in 1943 might have enabled the Western allies to beat the Red Army to the occupied countries of Eastern Europe, like Poland and Czechoslovakia.

ITALY

The creation of a massive base of operations in North Africa would, Churchill argued, provide the Allies with a staging post for the invasion of Italy, which he regarded as 'the soft underbelly of the Axis'.

In practice, the 'soft underbelly' was to prove a tough nut to crack but circumstances in 1943 seemed to favour Churchill's strategic preference rather than 'Operation Roundup'. This was because in July 1943 the Italian King Victor Emanuel III, who had connived at Mussolini's appointment in 1922, ordered his deposition. The alliance with Germany had never been popular in Italy, the entry into the war had been a disaster, and the Duce had become in his own words 'the most hated man in Italy'. Churchill assumed that the Germans would accept the Italian capitulation that followed Mussolini's overthrow. By then Sicily had fallen to the Allies (although there was an example of rather ridiculous Anglo-American feuding between General Patton and Montgomery) and a progression up the Italian peninsula with a friendly population seemed an enticing prospect.

In the event, Hitler did not react as Churchill expected. Just about the only promise that the Führer kept in his political career was that he would protect and support his friend the Duce. German paratroopers were sent to rescue the possibly rather reluctant Mussolini from his mountain-top imprisonment, and Wehrmacht formations raced southwards to seize strategic points in Italy before the Allies could capture them, including Rome. Thereafter the 'soft underbelly' thesis proved to be total illusion as the Anglo-American armies became involved in bloody slogging matches like Monte Cassino, and an aborted invasion of Anzio.

THE BOMBING OFFENSIVE

In the dark days of 1941, before America came into the war and the USSR was fighting desperately for self-preservation, Britain had few means at its disposal to hit back at Germany. One of them was the offensive by RAF Bomber Command against Germany's industrial heartland in the Ruhr, and later against major cities like Hamburg and Berlin.

Britain had suffered severely in the Lüftwaffe bombing offensives of 1940–2, even if the damage inflicted was far less than pre-war theorists had predicted, and there was a natural desire for revenge. Churchill shared this emotion, and the instrument for revenge was Air Marshal Sir Arthur 'Bomber' Harris, a fervent advocate of the effectiveness of so-called 'terror bombing' since the pre-war days when he had bombed rebellious Kurds in Mesopotamia.

There were 1000 bomber raids on Germany's great industrial centres, and in August 1943, the Air Staff calculated that 74 per cent of Hamburg and 54 per cent of Cologne had been flattened in raids. There is no doubt that the bomber offensive did force the Germans to build fighters rather than bombers, relocate their industries, spend massively on air defences and reorganise and delay their V rocket programme.

But the bomber offensive against Germany could not win the war single-handedly or obviate the need to invade continental Europe as Harris believed. Neither did it break the morale of the German people. In fact it sharpened hatred against the bombers and there were attempted lynchings of captured Allied flyers. Losses were consistently heavy as German night-fighters took a heavy toll of RAF bombers. RAF bomber pilots had the worst rate of loss of any section of the British armed forces in the Second World War.

Was there an alternative? The Americans favoured pinpoint precision bombing of key industrial sites like the ball-bearing factories at Schweinfurt, and much damage was done. Indeed Hitler's Armaments Minister Albert Speer expressed surprise in his memoir *Inside the Third Reich* that these raids were not persevered with. But Harris remained convinced that the 'terror' raids would break German morale. Thus the famous 'Dambuster' raid of 1943 was a unique event which did succeed in partially crippling the Ruhr dams but, in the Air Marshal's view, used up too many valuable resources. While it is clear that terror bombing of German cities did not achieve its objective, it is not clear that precision bombing was precise enough to decisively cripple German industry.

Churchill's attitude to the air war over Germany can at best be described as ambivalent. At times he appeared to share Harris' conviction that Bomber Command and the USAF could win the war single-handed. In 1941 he told the War Cabinet that 'Bombers alone provide the means of victory' (a remark reminiscent of his old adversary Baldwin), but he soon veered away from this stance to tell the Air Staff that 'German morale will crack and our bombing will play a very important part in bringing the result about'. Later, when thinking about his stated aim to 'de-house' the German civilian population, Churchill had pangs of conscience. 'Are we beasts?' he said. 'Are we taking this too far?' Critics might point out that Churchill did very little to interfere with Harris' strategy. The Air Marshal is remembered for his famous remark that the Germans must 'reap the whirlwind' for initiating the bombing of cities. But Churchill spoke in similar terms to his colleagues about the Germans: 'Let 'em have it. Remember this. Never maltreat the enemy by halves.' However, this remark goes largely forgotten, while that by Air Marshal Harris has passed into the lexicon of those historians, churchmen and politicians who questioned the morality of the bombing offensive.

Dresden

Much of the debate about the bombing offensive has focused on one terrible raid on the city of Dresden in February 1945. At this stage the war was won, and the devastation inflicted on this ancient and cultured city seemed superfluous and almost barbaric.

Why was Dresden bombed? In part, perhaps, to please Stalin by terrorising the German population and lessening resistance to the Red

Army. Certainly the city had no great strategic value. In his excellent history of the Second World War, Mark Arnold Foster concludes that: 'The main reason that Dresden suffered rather than some other German towns seems to have been that it was about the right size and that it had not been attacked before.'

Churchill does not emerge from the Dresden episode with any credit. As many as 125,000 German civilians may have died in the Dresden raid yet when he was asked about it after the war, Churchill replied, 'I cannot recall anything about it. I thought the Americans did it. Air Chief Marshal Harris would be the person to contact.' At best Churchill was being economical with the truth here because the available evidence suggests that, although approving the raid, he (like the American air force generals) subsequently tried to distance himself from its awful consequences.

The whole issue of the bombing offensive against Germany remains controversial as does Churchill's role in approving it. Understandably Bomber Command veterans remain profoundly resentful of the comparisons made between their raids on Germany and the depraved atrocities committed by the Nazis at Dachau, Belsen and Auschwitz.

OPERATION OVERLORD

By the beginning of 1944 even Churchill could not deny the imperative behind the need to invade France, take the strain off the Red Army and bring the war to a victorious conclusion. He continued to be obsessed with Italy and the campaign there which Norman Rose notes he endowed with 'an almost mystic quality'. He was therefore depressed by the failure of the Anzio landing (designed to lead to the capture of Rome). Being forced to remain on the defensive in Italy, said Churchill, 'is I think disastrous'.

Meanwhile Churchill presided over a special Cabinet committee dealing with the projected invasion of northern France code-named 'Overlord'. The vital requirement for 'Overlord' was surprise. The Germans had to be made to believe that the main landing was going to take place in the Pas de Calais, the shortest Channel crossing, whereas, in fact, it was to take place in Normandy. Intricate deception plans involving dummy camps, dummy aerodromes, false armies and bogus radio traffic succeeded admirably in deceiving the Germans.

Churchill approved the appointment of Eisenhower as Supreme Allied Commander for the invasion of France in June 1944. In view of their much larger contribution this post had to go to an American, but he was oddly pessimistic about the capacity of Anglo-American generals to defeat the Germans. Montgomery, in many respects Churchill's favourite general after Alexander, was scathingly written off by the Prime Minister who remarked that 'He will need 13 divisions before he'll ever make a move'.

The Prime Minister had referred to El Alamein in a celebrated broadcast as 'the end of the beginning'. The D-Day invasion that began on 6 June meant that the end after nearly five years of bloody conflict was in sight. At least in Europe.

THE FAR EASTERN THEATRE

Pearl Harbor was followed in the Far East by months of unmitigated disaster for the Anglo-American alliance. Three days after Pearl Harbor the two capital ships HMS *Repulse* and HMS *Prince of Wales* were sent out without adequate air cover and sunk by Japanese fighters. Malaya, the Dutch East Indies, Hong Kong and the Philippines all fell to a foe deemed to be no match for the white man and often in humiliating circumstances. Worst of all for Churchill personally was the loss of Singapore early in 1942 with its garrison of 130,000 to a Japanese landward attack. Churchill and the military planners had assumed that Singapore was still secure and its rapid fall (the latest 1995 study on this is aptly entitled *Singapore. The Pregnable Fortress*) was a tremendous blow to British prestige in the Far East.

It was agreed with Roosevelt that the Americans should have the dominant role in the Pacific. Churchill appointed Lord Louis Mountbatten as Supreme Commander South-East Asia and he found a good general in Slim whose 'forgotten army', the 14th, drove the Japanese out of Burma. Their attempt in 1944 to invade British India was seen off at Imphal and Kohima, and this threat never reasserted itself.

In the meantime the Americans under General Douglas MacArthur reconquered all the Pacific island chains until the fall of Iwojima in 1945, which put their super-fortresses (B29s) within range of the Japanese home islands. By then it was only a matter of time before Imperial Japan was brought to its knees.

timeline	1941	June	Hitler invades the USSR. Churchill pledges assistance to the Russians
		December	Pearl Harbor. US enters the war
	1942	February	Surrender of Singapore
		June	Fall of Tobruk
		August	Dieppe Raid
		October	British victory at El Alamein
		November	'Operation Torch'
	1943	January	Casablanca Conference
		May	'Dambuster' raid against the Moehne and Eder Dams
		July	Fall of Mussolini. Invasion of Italy
		October	USAF raids on Schweinfurt
	1944	June	'Operation Overlord' (D-Day) launched
		September	Failure of Arnhem Operation
		December	Failure of last German offensive in the Ardennes
	1945	February	Allied raid on Dresden
		May	Surrender of Nazi Germany

Points to consider

1) 'A complete dictatorship.' Do you agree with this description of the Churchill War Cabinet?
2) Was the campaign in Greece and Crete in 1941 an example of another ill-fated Churchillian 'sideshow'?
3) What major differences arose in strategical perception between Churchill and the US military in the Second World War? How did they affect the course of the war?
4) Can Churchill be accused of hypocrisy in the conduct of the RAF bombing offensive against Germany 1942–45?
5) How significant was Churchill's personal relationship with Stalin and Roosevelt in the winning of the Second World War?

12

'DOMESTIC POLICY AND DEFEAT'

Winston Churchill never disguised the fact that his priorities during the war were diplomatic and military rather than domestic. Nevertheless the Churchill wartime administration did preside over significant changes in British society. But how significant were they, and did the war create a 'consensus' among the British political parties about the need for reform in the post-war world?

THE 'CONSENSUS' DEBATE

The first point to note about the management of Britain during the Second World War is the increase in the powers available to the state whereby men and women of all classes were told where, and at what, they were to work. (Middle-class public schoolboys, for example, might become 'Bevin boys' – temporary coalminers – while their female equivalents might end up in a munitions factory or as part of the 'Land Army'.)

Churchill's role in British domestic policy during the Second World War was rather remote. On occasions he intervened, for example, to order the rather chaotic and probably premature imprisonment of British fascists on the Isle of Man in 1940, but the day-to-day management of the economy and social policy rested with others. In practice this meant that Attlee as Lord President of the Council and Churchill's wartime deputy headed a committee which ran these areas of government policy. Churchill headed the Defence Committee of the Cabinet which was responsible for the running of the war.

Did Churchill's preoccupation with running the war as head of the Defence Committee cause him to neglect domestic reform, or was this merely a consequence of actual disinterest in socio-economic issues? Kevin Jeffreys in his 1991 study *The Churchill Coalition and Wartime Politics, 1940–1945*, accuses Churchill of refusing to give a strong lead in domestic politics, seriously underestimating the electorate's desire for reform after the war, and contributing to a general malaise and complacency in the wartime Conservative Party. In the summer of 1945 the *Economist* (hardly a radical organ) commented that: 'With the single exception of one single election broadcast more than two years ago, Mr Churchill has been consistently contemptuous towards the need for reform.'

The main proponent of the consensus argument has been Paul Addison. He refers to the 'common ground' on social and economic policy which had been achieved by 1945. Addison points out that Churchill, who was 'physically and mentally exhausted' before the D-Day invasion was launched, had more time from the autumn of 1944 to apply himself to domestic issues which had always concerned him since his days as a Liberal reformer. Churchill himself, according to Addison, believed that there *was* a consensus between the parties on social issues and for this reason, Churchill wished to preserve the Coalition much as Lloyd George had been able to do at the end of the First World War, arguing that 'The partnership has been a successful one. Why dissolve it now?'

This 'if it isn't broken, don't mend it' argument didn't impress the Labour leaders who may well have remembered the fate of Lloyd George's coalition Liberals. More relevantly, according to Kevin Jeffreys, they wanted an early general election because they had distinctively different positions on socio-economic policy from the Tories.

The Beveridge Plan

The kernel of the consensus debate is the attitude of the two parties to the 1942 Beveridge Plan. Beveridge was a Liberal who had actually worked with Churchill as a civil servant when the latter was a Liberal minister. But, given the task of coming up with a comprehensive review of social policy, Beveridge's Plan to introduce free health care, compulsory insurance and unemployment benefit had features which Churchill disliked. He was alarmed by the potential cost of the Plan, but also had a fundamental difference of principle with Beveridge. The Plan recommended providing a minimum standard of support for *all* classes in the event of sickness or unemployment, whereas Churchill wanted assistance to go only to the working class with something equivalent to the old Poor Law as a further 'safety net' for the really disadvantaged in society. Under Beveridge's provisions, the Poor Law would be gradually phased out. Addison argues that it was 'not inconsistent for Churchill, as a pioneer of one type of welfare state to resist the introduction of another'. He also points out that the Tories were divided on the Beveridge Plan.

Kevin Jeffreys remarks that it was not intended that Beveridge 'should produce a major blueprint for social reform'. What he did produce was a 'cradle to the grave' scheme for a comprehensive system of social security, but one which would only work if it went hand-in-hand with a new, 'free at the point of delivery' health service, and full employment. According to Jeffreys the Conservative coalition ministers, particularly Kingsley Wood, the Chancellor of the Exchequer, objected to Beveridge on the grounds that he took no account of an unknown post-war situation and that people's expectations of a 'New Jerusalem' might be unrealistic. Labour by contrast are said to have supported Beveridge (apart from Herbert Morrison) while remaining anxious lest coalition unity be splintered by its implementation. So the Plan was shelved during the wartime period with no possibility of legislation.

A public opinion poll at the time of the Beveridge Plan's publication in 1942 showed that 86 per cent of those polled favoured the adoption of the Plan while only six per cent were opposed. This support, surprisingly perhaps, cut across all class boundaries and Churchill had always shown a keen appreciation of the need to assuage public opinion (within clearly defined limits). Was he therefore as negative on Beveridge and the reform process as Jeffreys suggests? He may have called Beveridge 'a windbag' but this proves nothing. (Ernest Bevin could not stand him either, and speedily despatched him from his earlier post at the Ministry of Labour.)

Churchill, as Addison points out, supported the idea of a National Health Service and educational reform and 'a broadening field for State ownership and enterprise'. He accepted Treasury reservations about open-ended financial commitments (he had not been a Chancellor of the Exchequer for nothing!), but promised a 'Four Years Plan' for reconstruction after Nazi Germany had been defeated.

If we accept the Addison analysis there may be much to be said for the consensus view. Churchill and the Labour leadership wished to preserve the Coalition (although Labour's motive was different – it expected to lose any election held too close to the end of the war). It is important to note that Labour rank and file wanted a break with the Tories, and that (Addison suggests) this put pressure on their ministers to achieve something in the way of constructive reform to retain their authority over that rank and file.

The other part of the argument focuses therefore on whether there *was* significant reconstruction and reform during the war. Kevin Jeffreys is unimpressed in his reference to the 'faltering steps' towards meaningful reform which underlines the essentially conservative nature of the achievement of the Coalition.

The 1944 Education Act

What was the nature of this achievement? Beveridge was, as its title suggests, a plan, not for implementation during wartime conditions. But a substantial educational reform, the work of R.A. Butler, was introduced in 1944. This raised the school leaving age to fifteen, made religious instruction compulsory and provided for selection between more academic grammar schools and secondary moderns at the age of eleven. Butler observed that the Tories seemed to have little real interest in educational reform (certainly Churchill did not), but the 1944 Act was still a significant educational watershed nonetheless.

The Town and Country Planning Act

The 1944 Town and Country Planning Bill was to have given local authorities the right to compulsorily acquire land at 1939 values, in the interest of rebuilding bombed out areas. Conservatives had an ideological objection to the compulsory purchase of land as Addision concedes. But backbench opposition was also aroused because agricultural land had gained in value during the war, and Tory landowners objected to losing capital gains in this way. For once, Churchill sided with the squirearchy and increases in compensation were agreed, although the Labour ministers were antagonised.

Conclusion

The consensus debate is heavily nuanced and complex, and it has not been possible here to acknowledge fully the contribution made by other historians.

Two major conclusions can perhaps be posited. Firstly, the legislative achievement of the Coalition is not all that impressive. This seems to back up the anti-consensus argument. Secondly, however, we must raise the question of whether in wartime conditions it is reasonable to expect wholesale and fundamental domestic reform. Plans were certainly made for the post-war period which did achieve a degree of cross-party support and even (arguably) the approval of Churchill. But was it the war which brought about consensus or the acceptance of post-war realities about reconstruction as Kevin Jeffreys suggests? The debate goes on.

Churchill receiving the plaudits of the crowd, 8 May 1945. Left to right: Oliver Lyttelton, Ernest Berin, Churchill, Sir John Anderson, Lord Woolton and Herbert Morrison

ELECTORAL DISASTER

Because of the popularity of Churchill as a war leader it was taken for granted that he would win the 1945 general election for the Conservatives. Churchill shared this view. 'They know they can't win without me,' he said of his not always loyal supporters.

By May 1945, the German war machine had collapsed, Hitler had committed suicide and Germany had surrendered unconditionally. Churchill, as indicated before, had wanted the wartime Coalition to continue but the Labour leadership, now responding to grass-roots pressure, pressed for a dissolution. In order to get in the vote from Britain's widely spread servicemen, there was to be a three-week gap between polling day and the declaration of the result.

In his highly readable contribution to the *Age of Austerity 1945–51*, Anthony Howard recreated the flavour of the second great electoral upset (after 1906) in twentieth-century British political history. The press, he points out, were largely convinced that Churchill's victory was inevitable. 'We are winning' said a *Daily Express* headline, and the Conservative candidate in Jarrow (of all places with its echoes of the 1936 Hunger March and Ellen Wilkinson's book *The Town That Died*) telegraphed to Churchill that Tyneside would like to touch 'the hem of your garment' in gratitude.

Yet an undercurrent of discontent with the Tories had long been present, and from 1942 Labour had been winning by-elections with ominous ease. Attlee had to be prevailed upon to speak in support of Coalition candidates, and Ackland's radical 'Commonwealth Party' polled impressively too. This trend was not just to do, as Harold MacMillan suggested, with 'the shadow of Neville Chamberlain' but with the folk memories of mass unemployment in the 1930s and a genuine desire for change. The assumption, therefore, that the veneration for Churchill as a war leader would condition responses in the poll proved to be a total illusion. The slogan 'the man who won the war' which had worked so well for Lloyd George in the 'khaki election' of 1918 was not going to work for Churchill in 1945. Lord Woolton, the Tory Minister for Food in the Coalition and a very shrewd political operator, advised the Conservative Party to highlight its post-war plans for housing and employment but he was ignored. Instead Addison says: 'Churchill decided that it would be a more effective tactic to frighten voters away from Labour.'

The 'Gestapo Broadcast'

In playing this old card which he had made such extensive use of in the 1920s, Churchill made one of the worst blunders of his entire political career.

On 4 June Churchill made a BBC broadcast in which he attacked the 'socialists' (as he always insisted on calling the Labour Party) and warned an incredulous audience that 'some form of Gestapo, no doubt very humanely directed in the first instance' would result from a Labour victory. It was difficult to recognise Clem Attlee, Ernest Bevin, Herbert Morrison or any of the other patriotic Labour ministers in this absurdly over-the-top diatribe. Why therefore did Churchill do it? Was he, as Addison suggests, under the influence of Professor Hayek's *The Road to Serfdom* (1944) which he had just read, and which suggested that centralised planning led inevitably to totalitarian government? Or was he, as Norman Rose speculates, just hopelessly out of touch with the mood of the moment? Thereafter Churchill tried to touch a more positive note but it was too late. The election results which were declared on 26 July revealed an overwhelming Conservative rout, and even Churchill's 20,000 majority at Epping fell by 3000 votes.

Party	Votes	Seats	% vote
Conservatives	9,988,306	213	39.8
Liberals	2,248,226	12	9.0
Labour	11,995,152	393	47.8
Others	854,294	22	2.8
Electorate: 33,240,391		Percentage turnout: 72.7	

Table 5: 1945 Election Result

Part of the reason at least for the overwhelming Tory defeat was, as Anthony Eden later wrote in his memoirs, that while there had been 'much gratitude to W[inston] as war leader, there is not the same enthusiasm for him as PM'. Churchill was not the first, or the last, British politician to underestimate the importance of bread-and-butter issues *vis à vis* the grand politics of the globe. In the meantime, as he himself observed, he had received the 'order of the boot' from the British electorate, while declining the Order of the Garter from King George VI.

timeline	1942 December	Publication of Beveridge Plan
	1944 February	Education Act Passed
	1945 June	Churchill's blunder in 'Gestapo' broadcast
	July	Tories heavily defeated in 1945 election. Churchill admits that he has got 'the order of the boot'

Points to Consider

1) 'Contemptuous towards the need for reform.' Is this a fair assessment of Churchill's domestic wartime record?

2) Was there a wartime consensus between the Conservative and Labour parties?

3) Why did the Conservatives suffer such a heavy election defeat in July 1945?

13

TWILIGHT

When the Second World War was over and he was also without office, Winston Churchill confessed that he was 'very lonely without a war'. Everything seemed to be an anti-climax and Clementine wanted him to retire from politics altogether. Some historians like John Charmley have argued that it would have been better for Churchill's reputation if he had retired after the Labour landslide in July 1945. But foreign affairs and the problem of dealing with Britain's erstwhile ally Soviet Russia kept Churchill's interest in politics alive, and brought him a second peacetime term as Prime Minister in 1951 and a final grudging retirement in 1955.

COLD WAR WARRIOR?

Once the Anglo-Americans had landed on the Normandy coast in June 1944 it was clear that the days of the Third Reich were numbered, as the Red Army pushed into Eastern and Central Europe. There were setbacks, notably in September 1944 when an attempt to seize the bridges over the Rhine failed at Arnhem and in December 1944 when the Germans briefly broke through in the Ardennes, but Churchill now had to turn his thoughts towards peacemaking, and the shape of the post-war world. He probably did so with some reluctance given his obsession with military matters, but he remained convinced that he could do business with Stalin personally. 'If only' he once remarked, 'I could dine with Stalin once a week, there would be no trouble. We get on like a house on fire.' The accuracy of this observation was put to the test in October 1944 when Churchill visited Moscow and discussed the post-war settlement in

Europe with the Soviet dictator. This was the occasion when the infamous 'naughty document' or percentages deal was agreed.

At an early stage in an extended visit, Churchill produced half a sheet of paper. On it were the names of all the Balkan states and the percentage interest in each deemed appropriate by Churchill for the USSR and Britain. In respect of Romania, Churchill had suggested a 90 per cent interest for the USSR with 10 per cent for Britain. Greece was to be the reverse – a 90 per cent interest for Britain and a 10 per cent interest for the USSR. In Bulgaria the relative interest was split 75/25 in favour of the Soviet Union while in the cases of Hungary and Yugoslavia, the division was to be 50 per cent each. Churchill later described how Stalin looked at the list, studied it, 'took his blue pencil and made a large tick on it and passed it back'. After this there was a long silence. The pencilled paper lay in the centre of the table. Eventually Churchill said:

> Might it not be thought rather cynical if it seemed we had disposed of these issues, so fateful to millions of people, in such an off-hand manner. Let us burn the paper.

Stalin allegedly replied, 'No, you keep it.' This so-called 'naughty document' formed the basis for the Yalta Agreement some months later.

POLAND

But Poland remained a sticking point. Churchill was outraged by the failure of the Red Army to assist the Warsaw Uprising against the occupying Germans in September 1944 (in circumstances which remain controversial as an offensive had carried the Russians to the outskirts of the city – the suspicion remained that it reflected a cold-blooded strategy of Stalin's). However, he found himself in a very difficult position over Poland. For three years, the Red Army had carried the weight of the Allied effort against Nazi Germany, and Stalin wanted control of Poland to fall to his 'Lublin Committee', a Polish Communist-inspired front. The AK (the Polish home army) was largely non-Communist and it was this force which was butchered by the Germans in September. Lastly there was the Polish government-in-exile in London, which had proved troublesome to Churchill in its insistence that Poland be restored with its pre-1939 boundaries.

Churchill became infuriated with 'the bloody Poles' when the Prime Minister of the government-in-exile, Mikolajcyk, refused to accept the former Curzon Line dating back to 1920–21. At one point he shouted at the Polish leader, 'Unless you accept the frontier you're out of business forever!' Mikolajcyk refused to budge but so did Stalin. The Soviet leader insisted on retaining the Polish territory annexed by the USSR in 1939, and compensating Poland by moving her western frontier to the Oder-Niesse Line inside Germany.

YALTA

In February 1945 the 'Big Three' Stalin, Roosevelt and Churchill met in the Crimea at Yalta to discuss the shape of the post-war world (Stalin rarely agreed to leave Soviet territory). At Yalta the 1944 'percentage deal' was given formal shape. A protocol agreed in 1944 to set up Occupation Zones in Germany was formalised, and the voting arrangements for the new United Nations, successor to the ill-fated League were agreed. In addition, the USSR gave a pledge to enter the Far Eastern war within three months of the end of the war in Europe. But on Poland Stalin adamantly refused to shift his ground.

The promise extracted by Churchill and Roosevelt that free elections should be held in liberated Eastern Europe was never to be kept. By 1948 Poland, Hungary, Bulgaria, Romania and Czechoslovakia were all to have Communist governments within the Soviet sphere of influence. In the lexicon of the traditionalist historians of the Cold War between East and West, Yalta was a 'sell-out' as bad as Munich for which Churchill bore a major responsibility.

Norman Rose summarises the traditional view that at Yalta:

United States' policy floundered in the hands of its mortally stricken President: the British hamstrung by their hopelessly gullible American partners, were powerless to foil the machinations of the Soviets.

Roosevelt was certainly a dying man at Yalta, but one who upset Churchill by marginalising him and courting Stalin, and Churchill, according to a leading Foreign Office observer, was 'a silly old man . . . knew nothing whatever of what he was talking about'.

Was Churchill duped at Yalta? It seems unlikely that he was, given that he had expressed anxieties about Soviet intentions as far back as 1943. Yet he continued to blow hot and cold about the USSR, as Martin Kitchen suggests, telling Colville after Yalta that 'Chamberlain had trusted Hitler as he was now trusting Stalin'. Clearly he *wanted* to trust Stalin but once the two men were apart, his old suspicions about the USSR began to reassert themselves.

Britain was also in an appallingly weak financial situation (see the table below). By the time of Yalta, Churchill himself was beginning to come to terms with exactly what this decline in economic and financial power meant. 'What a small nation we are,' he mused after the conference. 'There I sat with the great Russian bear on one side . . . and on the other the great American buffalo, and between the two sat the poor little English donkey.' And the 'little donkey' carried less and less clout in the international arena.

The economic cost of the Second World War for Britain

Overseas assets sold off or lost	£4,200 million
External debt	£3,300 million
Total loss	£7,500 million

Equivalent to 25 per cent of UK's national wealth

Source: Norman Rose, *Churchill. An Unruly Life*

Norman Rose absolves Churchill of any responsibility for a cynical sell-out to the USSR at Yalta. It was, he says, an agreement which was an inevitable result of the realities of *realpolitik* which had long preceded the conference itself. 'In the long run,' writes Rose, 'there was nothing he could have done'. Stalin's dominance of Eastern Europe was built into the exigencies of the wartime situation. David Reynolds agrees that Roosevelt and Churchill did not connive at the post-war Soviet domination and that their aim at Yalta was 'to prevent a legitimate sphere of influence from becoming a closed Stalinist bloc'. They failed, but that failure does not in any way prove complicity in what happened to the unfortunate Poles, Czechs, Hungarians *et al* after 1945.

Yet the doubts remain and Churchill was well aware of what had been gained and lost as a result of Yalta. Not for nothing did he call the last volume of his war memoirs *Triumph and Tragedy*. But it is worth noting that his parliamentary colleagues gave massive approval to the Yalta Agreement (396 votes to 25) at the time.

POTSDAM

Stalin's victory in the post-war settlement of Europe was confirmed at Potsdam in Germany two months after the Third Reich was finally defeated. The Polish-Soviet border was settled at the Curzon Line and the USSR was to get a quarter of the capital assets in its zone of occupation (literally anything of value that was not bolted down). Four Ds were to be imposed on the defeated, brain-washed Germans: democratisation, de-nazification, de-industrialisation and de-militarisation, in an attempt to undo the effects of twelve years of fascist, militaristic propaganda.

Stalin was at a distinct advantage at Potsdam as Roosevelt had died in April and the new President Truman was green in international affairs (although he soon impressed Churchill with his toughness and a grasp of his brief). The results of the British general election were announced while the Conference was in session, and Churchill was a caretaker Prime Minister who had to take his eventual successor Attlee to Potsdam with him.

Churchill's performance at Potsdam was widely criticised (did he sense his impeding electoral catastrophe perhaps?) and he was accused, not for the first time, of talking the 'most irrelevant rubbish'. Such concessions as the West won at Potsdam were trivial. All foreign forces were supposed to be evacuated from Iran (Stalin subsequently tried to renege on this agreement), and British and US forces were to be allowed to occupy Vienna with the Red Army. Days after Potsdam the USSR honoured its pledge to enter the Far Eastern war.

THE FULTON SPEECH

In 1946 Churchill was invited to speak at the University of Missouri at Fulton, President Truman's home state. In this speech he warned against the spread of Communism in Eastern Europe in a memorable passage:

> From Stettin in the Baltic to Trieste in the Adriatic, an iron curtain has descended across the continent. [The phrase 'iron curtain', so

strongly associated with the speech was not original. Churchill had already used it in correspondence and so had Hitler's Propaganda Minister, Goebbels.] Behind that line all the capitals of the ancient states of central and eastern Europe – Warsaw, Berlin, Prague, Vienna, Budapest, Bucharest, Sofia, all those famous cities and the populations around them, lie in the Soviet sphere and all are subject in one form or another not only to Soviet influence but to very high and increasing measures of control.

The 'iron curtain' speech at Fulton was not, as it is commonly portrayed, a great watershed in the development of the Cold War between the USSR and the West. It has only attained this status retrospectively. At the time, by contrast, opinion polls showed that few Americans shared Churchill's sentiments and fervently wanted a return to pre-war isolationism.

Less well remembered, as Steven Ambrose has pointed out in his excellent study of US foreign policy *Rise to Globalism*, was Churchill's reference in the speech to the atomic bomb which he described as a 'god-willed' American possession. This remark infuriated Stalin who regarded it as a provocation to the USSR, and helped destroy the already feeble hopes for UN control of atomic weapons altogether.

Britain's junior status in nuclear matters was humiliatingly reasserted by the US MacMahon Act in 1946, which banned any nuclear co-operation even with allies (citing fear of espionage in Britain's nuclear programme).

THE SUMMIT WARRIOR

The shadow of the Cold War darkened with the announcement of Marshall Aid, and the Truman Doctrine in 1947, the 1948 crisis when Stalin tried to force the Western powers out of Berlin, and full-scale war in Korea in 1950. Yet despite this, Churchill retained his belief in summitry. When he returned to office in 1951, at the advanced age of 77, he was determined to try to resolve the nuclear issue by means of a personal meeting with Stalin. It never happened, and indeed it could be argued that Britain's explosion of its own nuclear device in 1952 worsened the problem by bringing to fulfilment the Labour Foreign Secretary Bevin's proud boast that he would have an atomic bomb 'with a bloody Union Jack flying on top of it'.

Yet there is something infinitely moving about Churchill in old age and poor health (after a serious stroke in 1953) trying to recreate the old wartime comradeship. After Stalin's death in March 1953 he became hopeful that the new Soviet leadership might play a more constructive role – especially as the USSR acted as co-chairman with Britain at the 1954 Geneva Conference which ended the French war in Indo-China.

The problem was the United States. President Eisenhower (who came into office at the start of 1953) flatly refused to entertain the idea of a summit with the Russians. When Churchill suggested going to Moscow alone Eisenhower even threatened him with trade restrictions and a cut-off in US aid. Ponting observes that Churchill, who had been an early Cold War warrior in 1946 and strongly supported Bevin's initiative to set up NATO in 1949, 'found that it was not easy to change the stance and modify the rhetoric of an alliance just to fit in with his new enthusiasm for dialogue'. Perhaps Churchill should be given some credit for trying to change the rhetoric. Ultimately however he failed to secure a summit and this was one of the reasons for his belated decision to stand down in 1955, allowing the frustrated Eden (for years the heir apparent) to enter Downing Street.

EUROPE

Churchill sent out equally confused signals about Europe where an impetus towards integration had been created by the common experience of defeat and occupation. Britain, of course, had not undergone such an experience but Churchill had falsely raised the hopes of European federalists by referring to 'a kind of United States of Europe'. In radical fashion Churchill also spoke of the need for 'partnership between France and Germany'.

This rhetoric encouraged leading European federalists like Monnet to see Churchill as a potential founding father of a European Union. However, Churchill never had any intention of integrating Britain into Europe. Once in office, his interest in European unity faded markedly and his Tory government would have no more to do with the nascent European Coal and Steel Community (founded in 1951) than its Labour predecessor. Some might blame Churchill for helping to create a fatal ambiguity about European integration which has persisted ever since in

Britain. For him anyway Empire and transatlantic links (as befitted an Anglo-American by birth) always took precedence over any links with Europe.

INDIA

The immediate post-war period also saw the conclusion of the lengthy process which Churchill had fought against tooth and nail in the 1930s. In August 1947 independence was conceded to India and Pakistan by the Attlee government in the teeth of Churchillian objection.

During the war, Churchill went through the motions of examining the question of Indian independence to appease his Labour coalition partners who largely favoured it. In 1942 he even sent Sir Stafford Cripps (whom he maliciously referred to as Sir Stifford Crapps in private conversation) on a mission to India to determine its post-war status while covertly trying to undermine it. Suspicions also remain that the British were deliberately trying to weaken the support for the Congress Party while supporting Muslim separatism and the demand of the Muslim League for a separate Muslim majority state or 'Pakistan'.

Ultimately the argument in favour of conceding independence to India and Pakistan was overwhelming. Financial weakness and overstretched resources meant that Britain had to leave. Even the appointment of Mountbatten (a relative of the royal family and an old friend) as last Viceroy of India could not persuade Churchill to accept the inevitable. 'Scuttle,' he told the House of Commons bitterly in March 1947, 'everywhere, is the order of the day.' Only years later was he sufficiently reconciled to the existence of an independent India to describe its first Prime Minister Nehru as 'the light of the East'.

THE TORY RECOVERY

Churchill was undoubtedly stunned by the 1945 defeat, as was his party, but remarkably the Tories had restored their electoral fortunes within five years. In the election of February 1950 the Labour overall majority had fallen to just six, and in October 1951, the Conservatives were actually returned to office. How did this come about and how much of the Conservative recovery can be attributed to Churchill personally?

To some extent the Tories gained from the exhaustion of their opponents who had been in continuous office since the wartime coalition was formed in 1940. Bevin and Cripps died in office, Attlee underwent a serious operation and these difficulties were compounded in 1951 by the resignation of the fiery Health Minister Aneurin Bevan over the issues of rearmament and payments for NHS dental care and spectacles.

After the wave of nationalisations between 1946 and 1948, Labour seemed to lose its way in mid-term. Indeed historians have pointed out that from 1947 onwards Gallup polls showed the two major parties to be neck and neck in terms of public approval. The electorate was undoubtedly tired of the controls extended from wartime to peacetime which meant endless queuing, rationing and outright misery during the awful winter of 1947 when coal stocks ran out. 'Shiver with Shinwell and starve with Strachey' was the motto of the day, the two being Minister of Fuel and Minister of Food respectively.

But in *The Age of Austerity 1945–51*, Geoffrey Hodgson warns about too negative a view of the Tory recovery, which owed much to a dramatic transformation of both the organisation and philosophy of the party: 'Recovering in bulldog style from the traumatic defeat of 1945, the Conservatives put their house in order.' The hero here was Lord Woolton who was appointed Party Chairman in 1946 and drastically overhauled the party machine to rid the Conservatives of their blimpish image.

Hand in hand with Woolton's practical organisational reforms went the work of R.A. ('Rab') Butler as Chairman of the Conservative Research Department (merged by 1948 with the Parliamentary Secretariat) whose task had been to brief the Opposition in Parliament on a daily basis. Many of the Research Department's young men in the 1945–51 period, Powell, Macleod and Maudling, were to achieve Cabinet office in the 1950s.

Churchill may have seemed a remote figure to these rising Tory stars. In 1949 he suffered a minor stroke, and found concentrated effort on political affairs difficult. But on a good day he could still be an immensely effective parliamentary performer, and one such day occurred during the debate on the nationalisation of the steel industry in 1950. In a telling phrase Churchill castigated the Steel Bill saying: 'It is not a plan to help our patient struggling people, but a burglar's jemmy to crack the capitalist crib.' Such islands of vigour and forceful intervention persuaded Churchill, despite the objections of colleagues, that he should remain as party leader. Nevertheless foreign affairs remained the focus of his attention in the opposition years between 1945 and 1951. It took rank-and-file pressure to persuade him to overhaul the party machine, formulate clear policy positions against more nationalisation and accept the creation of the National Health Service in 1948. In his biography of R.A. Butler, Anthony Howard describes Churchill's attitude to reform within the Tory Party as essentially negative. 'Policy-making was a dangerous business out of which advantage only normally accrued to one's political opponents, who were provided with targets to shoot at.'

On a physical level Churchill, 77 in 1951, lacked the stamina to maintain rigorous control of the party machine or policy initiatives although he could still make imperious interventions (providing, for example, a personal party manifesto in 1951, days before Butler was supposed to be unveiling the official Tory one). Thus Howard's judgement that Butler was 'the architect behind the rebuilding of the Tory Party's entire post-war fortunes' seems a fair one even if it somewhat plays down Woolton's role in this revival.

PRIME MINISTER AGAIN

Churchill was restored to office in October 1951 despite the fact that Labour had a larger share of the popular vote (see the table on p.145). Given the difficulties that Labour had faced in the aftermath of the Second World War, it was a far from overwhelming triumph as Kenneth O. Morgan observes. 'What is surprising,' he writes in *The People's Peace. British History 1945–1989* 'is that the defeat was so very narrow.' This reflected a prevailing distrust of Churchill amongst the working classes where memories of the General Strike remained vivid, and the perception of him still as a 'warmonger' (the *Daily Mirror* suggested that Churchill's finger should not be allowed on the nuclear trigger). Until 1954 therefore the return of another Labour government seemed a real possibility.

These factors help to explain the emollient nature of Churchill's second, peacetime administration. There was a pronounced emphasis on 'One Nation' Disraeli-style Toryism and the government was, in Morgan's words, 'corporate and centralist'. Little attempt was made to interfere with the achievement of the Attlee government and only two industries, steel and road haulage, were taken out of public ownership.

Party	Votes	Seats	% vote
Conservatives	13,717,538	321	48.0
Liberals	866,139	6	2.5
Labour	13,948,883	295	48.8
Electorate: 34,645,573		Percentage turnout: 82.6	

Table 6: 1951 election result

Industrial Relations

Nowhere was this consensus-style politics more evident than in the sphere of industrial relations where rhetoric and practice spectacularly failed to meet. For although the Tories talked in the 1950 and 1955 election campaigns of repealing the 1906 Trades Disputes Act, amending the law of picketing and having secret ballots for the election of trade union officials, no action was taken on their return to office.

To some extent this turnabout reflected Churchill's personal beliefs and attitudes. He was aware of his poor reputation with the working class but always had a grudging respect for trade union leaders like Ernie Bevin. This 'institutional respect' as Roy Jenkins calls it, appears to have influenced Tory industrial policy between 1951 and 1955 – most strongly perhaps in the appointment of Walter Monckton as Minister of Labour.

Churchill had known Monckton for years, and they had been especially close when both represented the King's interest at the time of the 1936 Abdication Crisis. But Monckton was no politician in the normal sense of the word. He lacked strong party affiliations and was, according to K.O. Morgan, 'a diplomat, even a fixer'. These fixing qualities were used to keep the unions happy by means of courts of inquiry which invariably recommended pay increases, and may have contributed to a rise in wage inflation in the Churchill years. Jenkins regards the Monckton appointment as 'a signal that all differences would be split, all disputes would be arbitrated, and the seeds of the great inflation would be sown'. But Monckton's policy was the embodiment of his Prime Minister's admonition to the 1951 Parliament that 'what the nation needs is several years of quiet steady administration'. For this is what Britain got in those years.

The Economy

The Tories promised 'a bonfire of controls' when they returned to power and the end of rationing was easily achieved (although the process of ending wartime controls had actually begun under Labour).

The management of sterling was a less easy matter. As Chancellor, R.A. Butler seemed to veer erratically between inflationary tax cuts and constraint. Ultimately his widely unpopular plan to let the pound float on the currency markets brought about his demotion to the sinecure post of Lord President of the Council (the ambitious Macmillan ensuring that it did not carry with it, as during the war, the title of 'Deputy Prime Minister'). Churchill presided over an acrimonious debate in Cabinet on the floating pound although, as Morgan underlines, his 'understanding of these matters was scanty'. However, his political instincts were strong enough to recognise the dangers implicit in Butler's strategy which the Chancellor himself accepted would lead to rising prices and higher unemployment. The latter in particular in the post-Keynesian world after 1945, when full employment was a matter of political consensus, was unacceptable. So too were the international implications of Butler's policy, given the dependence of Commonwealth countries on sterling.

In an effort, perhaps, to restore his standing in the Tory Party, Butler gave away £134 million in income tax cuts in the 1955 budget just before the general election. The Tories won the election but the cuts led to a collapse in Britain's balance of payments and a rise in inflation.

RETIREMENT

By then Churchill himself had left office having celebrated his eightieth birthday in 1954 (the Commons presented him with a portrait which Clementine so loathed that she destroyed it!). Arguably he had stayed on far too long after 1951. Two factors, it has been suggested, persuaded him to do so. Firstly the death of Stalin in March 1953 which gave him the prestige of being the only surviving member of the great wartime triumvirate. Secondly, the botched gall-bladder operation on Anthony Eden in 1953 which meant that he, some 22 years younger than the ageing Prime Minister, was actually in worse physical condition. This, despite the fact that Churchill himself had a third serious stroke in the same year (details of which were withheld from the public) and Butler was left to run the government.

Churchill himself recognised the seeds of his own decay, telling Butler in 1954 that he felt like 'an aeroplane at the end of its flight in the dusk, with the petrol running out, in search of a safe landing'. His foreign policy concerns, the lure of office and remaining doubts about Eden's fitness for the post of Prime Minister forced an irritable Foreign Secretary to wait impatiently for that 'safe landing'. It came, as it had to, in April 1955. Ironically the great self-publicist left office in the middle of a national newspaper strike when Monckton's emollient tactics had for once failed.

LAST YEARS

Winston Churchill remained in the House of Commons until 1959. Now in increasingly enfeebled old age, his appearances in the House of Commons, which he had first entered in 1900, were few and far between. His anxieties about his successor seemed to be justified in part by the events of November 1956 when Eden's attempt to regain control of the Suez Canal, nationalised by the Egyptian leader Nasser in the previous July, resulted in humiliation and precipitated withdrawal by the British forces.

Retired politicians' lives are rarely happy. Together with his declining physical health, Churchill was plagued by listlessness and depression. His last coherent words, one of his biographers reports, were 'I am so bored with it all.' This boredom, after the high excitement and relentless endeavour of his years in office, may explain Churchill's propensity in his last years for foreign holidays and cruises at the expense of sometimes unlikely well-wishers such as the Greek shipping magnate Aristotle Onassis. This has elicited some rather pompous criticism by writers like Ponting who have equated a luxurious lifestyle with Churchill's aristocratic tastes and lack of concern for the common man and woman. But Churchill was, after all, an aristocrat posing as the 'Great

Commoner'; and such criticism smacks of the sort of censorious puritanism which led to Churchill's great political opponent Aneurin Bevan being called 'a Bollinger Bolshevik' because of his liking for champagne and high life.

Winston Churchill died on 24 January 1965. He had been made a Knight of the Garter in 1953 but declined a dukedom on retirement from office in 1955. He chose to be buried alongside his parents at the parish church at Bladon, near Blenheim Palace where he had been born more than 90 years before. He was given a state funeral, the first commoner to be granted such a privilege since the death of the Duke of Wellington in 1850. Such was the measure of the man.

For 60 years, Winston Churchill had been at the heart of affairs in the British body politic. He had at various times been admired and despised, loved and hated (sometimes indeed arousing all these emotions simultaneously) in a bewildering kaleidoscope of a career. His contemporary political opponent and one-time deputy, Clement Attlee, said he was: 'The greatest Englishman of our time – I think the greatest citizen of the world of our time.' Thirty years on, Norman Rose reflected on how Churchill was, for all his flaws, a political giant 'so impregnable that he never ceased gazing down upon contemporaries and rivals'.

timeline

1945	February	Yalta Conference
	July	Potsdam Conference
	August	Atomic bombs dropped on Hiroshima and Nagasaki
	September	Japan surrenders
1946	March	The Fulton 'iron curtain' speech
	September	Churchill refers to 'a kind of United States of Europe' in Zurich speech
1947	March	'Truman Doctrine' pledges US assistance to all states threatened by Communism
	June	US Secretary of State Marshall's speech promising economic assistance to Europe
1948	July	National Health Service comes into existence
1949	March	NATO Treaty signed
1951	October	Conservative election victory. Churchill's second term as Prime Minister
1953	March	Death of Josef Stalin

1955 April	Churchill retires from politics
1956 November	Suez Crisis
1959 October	First British election in which Churchill has not been a candidate since 1900
1965 January	Death of Winston Churchill

Points to Consider

1) Was Yalta a 'sell-out'?
2) Assess Churchill's responsibility for the start of the Cold War.
3) What part, if any, did Churchill play in the Tory recovery between 1945 and 1951?
4) To what extent did Churchill's second government live up to his 1951 pledge to provide 'quiet, steady administration'?
5) 'The greatest Englishman of our time.' Does Winston Churchill deserve this description of his career?

14

CONCLUSION

Winston Churchill is open to the accusation that he was an intensely ambitious, self-absorbed careerist who often appeared to care little for the opinions or feelings of others. This may prompt the reflection that had he not possessed these characteristics he would never have achieved what he did.

THE PATERNALIST

Robert Rhodes James' observation that had Churchill died in 1939 he would have been regarded as a failure has a good deal of force. Certainly in his *own terms* he would have been a failure. Yet the record of achievement before the Second World War was far from inconsiderable. Churchill's role in the great reforming Liberal government before 1914 was a central one, even if his reforming zeal cooled from the moment when he became Home Secretary. He was essentially a paternalist anxious to better the lot of the ordinary worker out of a desire to improve national efficiency and preserve law and order, rather than out of any burning conviction that the working class was oppressed. We should not find this surprising. Churchill was an aristocrat who retained the attitudes and habits of an aristocrat apart from that formative period in his youth, when under Lloyd George's influence, he challenged the power of the propertied classes. His essential conservatism was evident during his period at the Treasury in the 1920s, when a desire to appear financially orthodox overrode his own doubts about the decision to return to the gold standard. Unlike his mentor Lloyd George, Churchill was a dourly orthodox Chancellor of the Exchequer.

THE WARTIME LEADER

Churchill's supreme moment came in 1940. As he himself observed it was as if his whole life had been a preparation for his assumption of supreme power at the time of greatest national peril.

Of course he doctored the historical record. Documents which showed his wartime leadership in a poor light were suppressed in Britain's official histories of the Second World War. It was not true that peace terms with Germany were never discussed in Cabinet in the summer of 1940 as Churchill suggested. It was not true either that he had the complete support of the naval staff for his controversial decision to attack the French fleet at Mers-el-Kebir.

Yet he could, as Richard Lamb points out in *Churchill as War Leader. Right or Wrong?*, be 'statesmanlike and admirable' in casting aside the fierce ideological hostility of a lifetime and supporting Russia in 1941. And he created a genuine sense of comradeship and commitment in a wartime coalition which contained other powerful personalities like Bevin, Beaverbrook, Bracken and Dalton. Ultimately Richard Lamb's judgement that 'Despite many blunders and hasty impetuous decisions, only one verdict is possible. He was a great wartime leader' is fair. With Churchill, like Cromwell, it was the man 'warts and all'.

The peacetime legacy of the Second World War and Churchill's role remains controversial. In *The End of Glory* John Charmley writes that: 'At the end of a war which had been fought to stop one power dominating the Continent, a situation existed in which just that had come to pass.' Arguably, Churchill was too accommodating about Stalin's demands between 1941 and 1943 and then too tardy in trying to dig in his heels over Poland in 1944–5. Charmley remarks that Churchill wanted to precipitate Britain into a war for which it was not ready in the 1930s, but what was the alternative? A Nazi-dominated Europe would hardly be more palatable than a Soviet-dominated one, and Britain in the end lacked the military clout to prescribe the shape of post-war Europe. The idea too that by avoiding a war in which, to use Baldwin's phrase, 'the Nazis and the Bolshies would knock hell out of one another', the British Empire would somehow be preserved seems gravely flawed. Churchill did after all spend a whole career vainly trying to resist the claims of nationalism in the Indian sub-continent and these claims did not disappear. Neither did the anti-imperialist sentiment in the United

States which made Churchill feel out of place in Roosevelt's White House. In this context it is Charmley, as much as Churchill, who appears to be a romantic. He believes that somehow the British Empire would have been preserved if Britain had stayed out of the Second World War, and left Germany and the USSR in a life and death struggle.

THE PEACETIME PREMIER

Churchill was a cautious consensual peacetime Prime Minister. In this he almost certainly reflected the national mood. The British people had suffered enough alarms and excursions in the previous decades.

Was he, as Roberts suggests, an 'appeaser' of the unions in a sense that was damaging to the overall interests of the British economy? Perhaps. But Roberts' analysis totally omits any reference to the failings of British management, the chronic longstanding failure of the City of London to invest in British industry, and the desire of the Churchill government to give the working classes (after many years of privation) a reasonable standard of living. His attempts to impugn the patriotism of the British working class by reference to the wartime strike record seem rather cheap. Churchill would never have been guilty of this, although he was capable of letting anti-socialist paranoia get the better of him. Weeks after saying that he was taking his 'friend Clem Attlee' to the Potsdam Conference, he made his notorious 'Gestapo' speech gaffe.

Roberts' attacks on Churchill's alleged 'racism' seem equally inappropriate. From the vantage point of the 1990s Churchill certainly had racist attitudes. He made offensive remarks about Gandhi and made clear his unwillingness to associate with blacks. In doing so, he was reflecting the attitudes and prejudices of his generation and its condescending imperialist assumptions. Hugh Dalton, for example, a radical socialist Chancellor in the Attlee government, is also on record as making offensive comments about black people. He was educated at Eton and Cambridge and was the son of George V's personal chaplain at Windsor. Yet Churchill could not accept him or other Labour public schoolboys as equals. It would have been surprising if, therefore, he had not also retained the ethnic prejudices of a youth spent in the heyday of the Raj.

In the end Churchill was his own man. He once said, 'I am an English Liberal. I hate the Tory Party.' He ratted on the Liberals but was never a comfortable bedfellow of the Tories either. He was certainly not the 'Winston' of Thatcherite legend, for his paternalism and latter-day collectivism were in no sense part of thrusting market-orientated Toryism. He could after all be moved to tears by the knowledge that people in blitzed-out London would queue for bird-seed (some said he cried too easily!).

Just as his father was hard put to define what 'Tory Democracy' meant, so Churchill might have had difficulty in explaining his political beliefs. The charge of ruthless egotism will, therefore, remain but the paradox is that no one seems quite able to explain how this allegedly ruthless egotist could attract such personal devotion. Perhaps Churchill was an adventurer, but as Addison points out: 'It was in his nature to believe in a land fit for adventurers to live in, and he imagined that his own conceptions of liberty and progress were shared by the mass of the people.' Often they were and often they were not. That, surely is the lot of political leaders in a democracy.

BIBLIOGRAPHY

The amount of reading material available on Churchill is daunting. This list is by no means exclusive but does include the texts referred to in the book, together with comments on their appropriateness for A Level students and first year undergraduates.

Addision, P., *Churchill on the Home Front.* (Pimlico, 1993). Essential for understanding of domestic aspects. Readable and accessible.

Blake & Louis (Eds.), *Churchill.* (Oxford, 1993). Contributions by Jenkins, Watt, Carver, Edmonds, Kimball et al. Essential reading for the more able A Level student and undergraduates.

Cameron Watt, D., *How War Came.* (Heinemann, 1989). For the more able only.

Carlton, D., *Anthony Eden.* (Unwin, 1986). Critical of its subject.

Charmley, J., *Churchill's Grand Alliance.* (Hodder and Stoughton, 1995). The latest study of the special relationship between Britain and the United States during the war years and the period up to the Suez Crisis.

Charmley, J., *Churchill. The End of Glory.* (Hodder and Stoughton, 1993). Too weighty for A level.

Charmley, J., *Chamberlain and the Last Peace.* (Hodder and Stoughton, 1989). Puts the arguments for appeasement and the Grand Alliance. Accessible to most able at A Level and first-year undergraduates.

Churchill, Winston, *My Early Life.* (Fontana, 1959). A rattling good yarn.

Churchill, Winston, *The Gathering Storm.* (Cassell, 1948). Essential for an understanding of the 'Churchillian critique' of appeasement.

Elphick, P., *Singapore. The Pregnable Fortress.* (Hodder and Stoughton, 1995). Specialist study.

Emerson, J.T., *The Rhineland Crisis.* (Temple Smith/LSE, 1977). Specialist study not accessible to A Level students.

Foot, M., *Aneurin Bevin* (2 vols). (Paladin, 1975). Specialist biography.

Foster, M. Arnold, *The World War.* (Fontana, 1976). Very readable and accessible for A Level students.

Gilbert, M., *Churchill. A Biography.* (Heinemann, 1991). Shortened version of massive multi-volume work. Still too detailed for majority.

Gilbert, M., *Winston Churchill. The Wilderness Years.* (Macmillan, 1981). Focus on 1929–39 period. Accessible to more able at A Level.

Harris, K., *Attlee.* (Weidenfeld and Nicolson, 1982). Specialist biography.

Hennessey, P., *Never Again.* (Jonathan Cape, 1992). Comprehensive on 1945–1951.

Howard, R., *RAB. The Life of R.A. Butler.* (Jonathan Cape, 1987). For the real enthusiast only.

Lamb, R., *Churchill As War Leader. Right or Wrong?* (Bloomsbury, 1993). Probably too detailed for the vast majority.

Morgan, K.O., *The People's Peace. British History 1945–89.* (Oxford, 1990). Readable general survey. For undergraduates and top A Level band.

Neville, P., *Neville Chamberlain. A Study in Failure?* (Hodder and Stoughton, 1992). Companion volume in the series.

Ponting, C., *Churchill.* (Sinclair Stevenson, 1994). Spoilt by its animus.

Reynolds, D., *Britannia Overruled.* (Longman, 1991). Very good survey of British foreign policy. Accessible to undergraduates and A Level students.

Rhodes James, R., *Churchill. A Study in Failure.* Detailed analysis of career up to 1939. Selected chapters useful.

Roberts, A., *Eminent Churchillians.* (Weidenfeld and Nicolson, 1994). Patchy and dogmatic.

Rock, W., *British Appeasement in the 1930s.* (Edward Arnold, 1977). Useful and accessible to top band of A Level students.

Rose, N., *Churchill. A Turbulent Life.* (Simon and Schuster, 1994). Readable and accessible.

Sissons, M. and French, P. (Eds.), *The Age of Austerity 1945–51.* (Penguin, 1963). Very useful compilation and accessible to most.

Taylor, A.J.P., *The Origins of the Second World War.* (Hamish Hamilton, 1961). Difficult reading for A Level students but immensely stimulating.
Taylor, A.J.P., *English History 1914–45.* (Oxford, 1975). Immensely readable as always. Accessible for first-year undergraduates and top range A level.

Useful Articles

Day, D., 'Churchill and his War Rivals', *History Today*, April 1991.
M. Gilbert, 'Winston Churchill', *Modern History Review*, Volume 4, Number 3, February 1993.
Kitchen, M., 'Winston Churchill and the Soviet Union during the Second World War', *Historical Journal*, 1987.

Audio Visual

Churchill. Commentary by Martin Gilbert. Much interesting archive film. BBC TV Video.
The World at War, Programme 4, 'Alone'. Focus on Great Britain in crisis of 1940. Thames TV Video. The multi-part series also contains much other useful material on Churchill in the overall context of World War Two.
Young Winston. Feature film starring Simon Ward as Churchill.

Index